COVE POINT
ON THE CHESAPEAKE

all the best,

Carol Booher

July 1, 2023

COVE POINT
ON THE CHESAPEAKE
The Beacon, the Bay, and the Dream

CAROL McCABE BOOKER

New Bay Books

COVE POINT ON THE CHESAPEAKE

by Carol McCabe Booker
Copyright © 2021
by Carol McCabe Booker
All Rights Reserved

Editor
Sandra Olivetti Martin
New Bay Books
Fairhaven, Maryland
NewBayBooks@gmail.com

Cover Design by Carol McCabe Booker

Interior design by Suzanne Shelden
Shelden Studios
Prince Frederick, Maryland
sheldenstudios@comcast.net

Cover Photo: Nathalie Wolkonsky with her cousin Alex Doubiago
at the Cove Point Lighthouse in the late 1940s. (Photo by Dimitri
Wolkonsky. Courtesy Wolkonsky family.)

A Note on Type: Cover and section heads are set in ITC Bookman
Std Open Type. The text font is ITC Bookman Std Open Type.

Library of Congress

Cataloging-in-Publication Data

ISBN 978-1 7348866 3 4

Printed in the United States of America

First Edition

DEDICATION

To our son, Teddy, who, like his parents,
has loved the Cove since first sight.

Table of Contents

To understand the shore, it is not enough to catalogue its life. Understanding comes only when, standing on a beach, we can sense the long rhythms of earth and sea that sculptured its landforms and produced the rock and sand of which it is composed; when we can sense with the eye and ear of the mind the surge of life beating always at its shores—blindly, inexorably pressing for a foothold.

PROLOGUE

The past is a lighthouse, not a port.

— Russian proverb

What if a lighthouse could capture its past—recording for posterity the dramas played out over the centuries in the sweep of its beam? The epic spun out by the Chesapeake Bay's oldest continuously operating beacon would be of larger-than-life heroism, tragedy, bliss and blunder against the backdrop of a fickle sea.

By the 1800s, watermen had experienced too many wrecks on the hidden shoals off Cove Point, the midpoint on the two-hundred-mile estuary stretching south from Havre de Grace, Maryland to Newport News, Norfolk and Virginia Beach in the Old Dominion. These seafarers were descendants of the watermen, farmers, tradesmen, adventurers, dreamers and schemers who had sailed across the Atlantic after a legendary explorer spread the word that the Chesapeake was "it." They petitioned the government for a lighthouse to warn the unaware, and in 1828 the tower was built and the beacon lit. Its site was the white sand beach jutting out into the Bay, like a pugnacious youth daring the northeast wind to hit it with all it's got. Cove Point had the kind of moxie that comes with unspoiled beauty, coupled with a history millions of years in the making.

South of the light was a quiet, crescent-shaped hollow with a wharf where slaves loaded ships with tobacco from local plantations. A century later, the wharf and plantations would be gone, and work-a-day city dwellers sixty or more miles away would be lured to the white sand beach and teeming fishery by the hype of newspaper ads rivaling Capt. John Smith's exuberance over the Bay's bounty.

Among the first, and least expected, was a Russian princess. Finding the forests of Cove Point enchantingly reminiscent of her pre-Bolshevik homeland, she set about to recreate a piece of that Old World. Less than a decade later, the U.S. Army rolled up to the beach cottages from ships with gaping bows, in a dramatic rehearsal for a wartime assault on Normandy. An audience of kids watched in wonder from the woods. When most of the remnants of rockets and shells were gone, a fortune hunter arrived to mine the north shore for a rare metal, financing the fiasco with the cash of Maryland residents. After the dismantling of that delusion, two industrial giants rose above the shoreline like more incongruous mistakes, three miles apart. Meanwhile, as if bearing witness to the Japanese proverb that darkness reigns at the foot of a lighthouse, a rip current struck randomly like a demon over eight decades, dragging the unwitting out to sea from the surf beneath the beacon.

Today, in the age of accelerated climate change, Cove Point has achieved its most dubious distinction: it is the place declared most flood prone along Calvert

County's entire Bay shore. The tiny community, nestled for almost a century between the heavens and the shifting sands, is now threatened as none other by sea levels rising three times faster than the worldwide average over the past two decades. For all its moxie, Cove Point is a fragile place, like Tangier Island and other historic bulwarks across the Bay, where the future is usually discussed in terms of decades rather than centuries.

Every community up and down the Bay's western shore has its story, woven out of dreams, adventures and misadventures. This is Cove Point's story. And like its signature lighthouse, it's one rife with warnings.

Cove Point on the Chesapeake

1

THROUGH THE EXPLORER'S EYES

Heaven and earth never agreed better
to frame a place for man's habitation.
—Capt. John Smith, 1608

The lean man with bushy beard and long, flowing hair couldn't have agreed more with the glowing assessment penned by the British explorer almost 300 years earlier when describing the shores of the Chesapeake Bay. Benjamin Catterton had nowhere near John Smith's experience or exposure to the world beyond the woods where he lived at Cove Point, near the tip of Calvert County in southern Maryland. But he knew what was good, and life here was very good.

Benjamin Catterton was a hermit. When county assessors stumbled upon him in October of 1896, he told them he had long lived in solitude, caring nothing for the outside world. Here on the Chesapeake Bay where stately pines grew tall and dense, forming a shelter even the sun could not pierce nor the winds penetrate, Catterton was "monarch of all he surveyed." He had never ventured even as far as the county seat at Prince Fredericktown, about seventeen miles north, and did not wish to do so. He had been to church only twice in his life, and had voted only twice, but each time his chosen candidate was defeated. He figured it wasn't worthwhile to vote any more.

Catterton and Smith reached their kindred conclusions about the Bay's idyllic shores from two very different perspectives. Catterton had never been beyond the southern half of rural Calvert County, while the British explorer had set foot on at least four continents before declaring the Chesapeake possibly the most pleasant place ever known. It was a site, he raved, where heaven and earth converged to frame a place perfectly designed for the enjoyment of humanity.

Smith backed up his striking assertions with descriptions of "large and pleasant navigable rivers" flowing invitingly into a huge estuary, surrounded by lands "not mountainous nor yet low but such pleasant plaine hils and fertle valleyes, one prettily crossing an other, and watered so conveniently with their sweete brookes and christall springs as if art it selfe had devised them."

On one of those rivers, he encountered the Pawtuxent, one of three Indian tribes living peacefully there, and more hospitable to the explorer and his crew than any others they met along the way. He returned the favor by naming the river after them. At least 100 feet deep in some places, the Patuxent (its modern spelling) also yielded an abundance of shellfish—oysters, clams and mussels—and a greater variety of diverse fish than he'd found elsewhere. Fish the Englishmen were able to identify included sturgeon, grouper, porpoise, mullet, trout, sole, shad, perch, rockfish, eels, lamprey, catfish, and herring. Smith found three species fascinating enough to describe specifically: the puffer, "which will swell till it be like to burst when it comes into contact with the air;" and what might have been the sea robin, a strange little fish he compared to medieval images of the dragon slain by St. George, just a small example of the exaggerations to which he was prone. The third was the stingray, whose tail, he later warned from personal experience, is very dangerous and so painful that he named the site of his encounter with the winged swimmer, near the village of Deltaville in Middlesex County, Virginia, Stingray Point.

Just north of the yawning mouth of the Patuxent, he sailed along the Bay's western shore, marveling at its line of sheer, striated cliffs, undulating between marshes and sandy beaches to heights as great as 100 feet, topped by dense forests, until eventually descending onto a white-sand beach in a tranquil cove the shape of a crescent moon. This natural harbor then ran northeast about three miles until the beach jutted out into the Bay, forming a point, Cove Point, as it would later be aptly named. Less than five nautical miles separated this cuspate foreland (the scientists' term for it) from the Bay's Eastern Shore. (For some unknown reason, that shoreline has always been capitalized, while the western shore often is not.) The span was so narrow that even without a telescope, a mariner could spy the falcons, sparrow hawks, and osprey soaring above either shoreline. It was also the approximate midpoint on the Bay, about eighty-four nautical miles south of the headwaters, and slightly more than that from its mouth.

Despite all his exuberance in documenting this exploration, the voyage up the Chesapeake was a disappointment to Smith, who had expected to find both a passage to the Far East and a wealth of gold.

Over the next two centuries, an endless flotilla sailed out of English ports in Capt. Smith's wake, following his charts across the Atlantic to the Chesapeake. Some brought with them impoverished families seeking a better life in the New World. Some carried religious minorities escaping persecution. Other voyagers had no qualms about persecuting anyone else they might encounter, even fellow colonists, whose views, religious or otherwise, differed from theirs. And less than a dozen years after Smith's exploration, the first of many ships carrying a chained cargo of human beings within their hulls would arrive at the mouth of the Bay. It was the shameful advent of slavery in America. And it would quickly become a major fact of life far beyond the shores caressed by the great Bay, spreading like a cancer until no less than civil war could excise it from an inflicted—and conflicted—national body.

A landmark on this passage north, Cove Point was not only a midpoint but also a geologic phenomenon on the Bay's western shore in what eventually became Calvert County, a narrow stretch of fertile, forested acreage bordered on the east by the Bay and on its south and west by the deep Patuxent River. Over time the area would become a magnet for paleontologists drawn by its prehistoric past, the millions of years during which the Atlantic slowly receded, leaving behind a graveyard of marine life in the abandoned seabed. When the force of river waters eventually carved out the country's largest estuary, the cliffs north and south of Cove Point were laden with fossils—shark teeth, whale bones, ray bars, dolphin vertebrae, and hundreds of other specimens—from the Miocene period, five to twenty-three million years ago. As these cliffs eroded at the mercy of northeasterly winds and tides, they shed their treasures for discovery by beachcombers in the sands along the shore. These explorers also found arrowheads and spear tips left behind by Native tribes who'd hunted in the dense forests, long before Capt. Smith's voyage. And they found artifacts from the Point's colonial history, when it was part of seventeenth century Eltonhead Manor, the largest manor ever granted by Maryland's Lord Baltimore.

The magnificent estate would have stretched over 5,000 acres from the marshes at Cove Point south along the Bay to Drum Point, at the mouth of the Patuxent. But it never came to fruition. The would-be lord of the manor wasn't able to meet the conditions of the grant, ultimately leaving the land for eventual sale to farmers in smaller parcels. An ad for one large parcel of 1,000 acres was placed in the *Maryland Gazette* newspaper (based in Annapolis) in the spring of 1790. It described the Bayfront acreage around Cove Point in superlative, if repetitive, terms, listing its 150 acres of excellent marsh, 100 acres of excellent meadow, an "excellent fishery" off the Point, and a "pond that furnishes very fine oysters." There were also "two thriving young apple-orchards," containing about 400 trees, "two tobacco houses" in good repair, and "several small houses for the accommodation of tenants."

A great proportion of the land was level, the ad continued, and well adapted to the culture of corn, wheat and tobacco, while the rest of the parcel abounded with "fine timber, oak, hickory, chestnut and pine," as well as a "sufficient stream for a grist and saw-mill." Topping it off, the owner promised, "There are few places that exceed this for wild-fowl."

Almost a century and a half later, newspaper ads hawking the attractions of Cove Point for Washington-area residents looking for a pleasant place to spend their summers, sunbathing on white sands, swimming in a tranquil cove, or enjoying water sports on the Bay, mentioned only one of the attributes listed in the 18th century ad—the excellent fishing.

Our story begins in the 1800s, when the bucolic setting at Cove Point saw a major change with the sale of a four-and-a-half acre parcel at its tip to the United States Government. On that site, in 1828, the government built a fifty-foot tall lighthouse. Topping the tower was an oil-fueled beacon intended to guide the ships that by then were passing the Point day and night, transporting people and goods between Baltimore, Norfolk, and beyond. For one reason or another, these schooners and steamers too often did not complete the journey safely; many ran aground or sank on the shoals around the Point. The neighboring cliffs offered protection from northwest winds, but coming too close posed greater risks. Beneath the surface on even the most tranquil day, the Point hosted hidden dangers worthy of every waterman's respect—and woe to those who ignored them.

2

THE BEACON

*This journal shall...include
a complete record of important events*
—Instructions for lighthouse keepers

When Congress appropriated $6,000 in 1825 for the installation of a lighthouse at Cedar Point, near the mouth of the Patuxent, Maryland's deepest river, many mariners protested. They argued that it made much more sense to position the lighthouse farther north at Cove Point. There, prevailing winds and daily tides, not to mention hurricanes and nor'easters, created shifting shoals, including a Cove Point "bar," stretching out toward the shipping lanes. These hazards lay in wait for unsuspecting navigators maneuvering past the red-clay cliffs to its north and south, often coming too close. So three years later, a new appropriations bill provided for the light to be built at Cove Point.

Despite the towering beacon, however, whether due to the shifting Bay floor or human error, the dramas that played out within its stunning view over the next century were the source of riveting newspaper accounts. The *Baltimore Sun's* coverage of the Bay began in 1837, while the *Evening Star* (at intervals the *Washington Star*) and *The Washington*

Post followed in 1852 and 1877; even more local, the weekly *Calvert Gazette* hit the beat in Prince Frederick in 1885. (Entering the scene decades later, the *Calvert Independent* had a seventy-year run from 1940 to 2011, while the *Calvert Recorder* was a late-comer in 1971.)

Many of the incidents the newspapers reported were collisions between schooners and steamers, each usually blaming the other for changing course at the last minute. Some of the accounts were terrifying despite their brevity, such as *The Sun's* one-paragraph report of the night of January 6, 1842, when the steamboat *Georgia*, en route from Baltimore to Norfolk, and directly abreast of Cove Point at 9:30 p.m. on a clear night, was struck on her starboard bow by the schooner *Pocahontas*:

> *Both boats were carrying lights, and Capt. Coffey of the Georgia, apprehending an encounter, had the bell rung, and hailed the Pocahontas as she stood on, but the latter boat was at the top of her speed, and the collision was thus rendered unavoidable.*

The smaller vessel was disabled and its captain seriously injured by a blow to his head from the *Georgia's* snapped flagstaff. The latter's captain beached his steamer at Cove Point, while his counterpart lay without medical aid until taken off by another schooner the next morning, along with his passengers. The *Pocahontas* was then towed to Baltimore, where the *Georgia* returned under its own steam. The consequences of the accident, the paper speculated, would be even more "serious" than its occurrence.

Just days before winter's end in 1859, "a tremendous gale" brought the brig *Kirkland*, carrying a cargo of sugar, ashore at Cove Point, where it was feared broken up. There was no mention of passengers on this ill-fated voyage. But there were other disasters that did cost lives. Under the screaming headline "COLLISION OFF COVE POINT—Lives of 100 Passengers in Danger, Fortunate Escape," the *Evening Star's* front page reported the collision of the steamer *George Leary* with the propeller ship *Sea Gull*:

> *The Leary was cut down to the water's edge, but the shifting of the freight forward lifted the injured part above water, and prevented her from sinking.*

While the *Leary's* passengers and freight were saved, the paper reported:

> *The chief steward was lost overboard, and the chambermaid and a deckhand were badly injured, the chambermaid it is supposed fatally.*

Sometimes the failure of vessels to navigate past the light was embarrassing to their sponsors, as in 1908 when the gunboat *Hist*, escorting a submarine flotilla from New York to the U.S. Naval Academy at Annapolis, ran aground off Cove Point. The *Evening Star's* report included no explanation for the mishap.

It was not unusual to find rewards posted in classified ads for the return of the body of a lost seaman. Relatives of the mate aboard the steamer *Lucille* placed one in January, 1869, after he went missing off Cove Point in a collision with a pungy, a type of schooner peculiar to the Chesapeake. Nearly two decades later, $100 was offered for recovery of the body of the captain of the schooner *Neptune*, who'd been knocked overboard by the mainsheet off Cove Point while jibing the mainsail.

THE DEEP FREEZE AND OTHER HAZARDS

The frigid winters of those decades brought another kind of danger. During the blizzard of February, 1895, the revenue cutter *Crawford* made front page news for its assistance to a number of vessels in distress on the Bay, including the steamer *Richmond*, grounded at the Cove Point wharf (in the bowl of the hollow south of the light) due to low water. Established under Treasury Secretary Alexander Hamilton in 1790, the Revenue Cutter Service's mission was to collect duty from ships importing goods into the United States. But since they were designed for speed, and able to travel into shallow waters, the cutters quickly proved their worth for other purposes as well, such as these rescues and numerous others in the Bay near Cove Point. Even so, these swift and agile patrollers of the Bay were sometimes snagged themselves on the shoals off the Point, as was the fate of the *Androscoggin*, shortly after leaving a repair dock in Baltimore en route to patrol duty in Portland, Maine, during an early morning January gale. Another cutter, the *Apache*, came to the rescue, setting it afloat with no apparent damage.

In 1912, the longest and most severe Chesapeake freeze on record brought navigation to a halt in parts of the Bay. The deep freeze hit in early January and settled in until mid-February. From Annapolis to Cove Point, the temperature dipped to around minus five degrees Fahrenheit, turning the Bay into solid sheets of ice six to ten inches thick. Daily press reports described foreign and domestic steamers surrounded by ice fields off Cove Point. The *Evening Star* in one report dramatically described tugs and barges laden with 10,000 bushels of oysters bound for Baltimore as "imprisoned" in the pack ice off the Point.

Later in the year, shipping interests lobbied the U.S. Weather Bureau to establish a weather signal station at the lighthouse, enabling shipping masters to keep posted as to probable changes in the weather. The only signal station of that type at the time was far south at Cape Henry, where a system of lanterns was displayed at night and flags during the day, telling of approaching changes. The shippers complained that two other stations at Cambridge and Annapolis were "so far distant from the regular course of vessels bound up and down the bay that they are of little practical use to masters of steam and sailing craft." The station was finally approved in 1920, after the Bureau of Lighthouses agreed that it would not interfere with its own work. The Weather Bureau called the establishment of the station, which would provide warnings 24 hours in advance of a storm, the most important improvement of the storm warning service on the Bay in recent years.

THE *THREE RIVERS*

By far the most heartbreaking tragedy caught in the steady sweep of the Cove Point Light during that first century occurred in the summer of 1924. The steamer *Three Rivers* (named for the Potomac, Patuxent and Rappahannock) was bound for Baltimore from Crisfield, in Somerset County on Maryland's Eastern Shore, on the Fourth of July with almost 100 passengers aboard. Around midnight an upper deck suddenly erupted in fire, its cause never determined. Dense smoke quickly filled the vessel and lower decks, threatening all with death from asphyxiation. Among the passengers were the fifty-nine members of the Baltimore *Evening Sun* Newsboys Band, a promotional vehicle organized by the paper in 1922. The teen band had given one of its very popular free concerts that day at the Chesapeake Bay workboat races in Crisfield. First word of the fire was telephoned to the Maritime Exchange in Baltimore from the Cove Point Lighthouse, reporting that other boats were hastening to the scene. But the *Three Rivers* was already burning from stem to stern.

Witnessing the conflagration from some six miles away, the steamers *Middlesex* and *Allegheny* raced full speed to the rescue, quickly pulling aboard some ninety survivors clustered on the *Three Rivers'* lower deck or thrashing about in the dark Bay waters. After thirty minutes of terror, ten passengers and crew, among them five of the boys, were deemed lost.

Later, Mrs. Mary Hall, the wife of *Three Rivers* Capt. Spencer Hall, a veteran mariner with many years experience on the Baltimore route, said he had had a premonition of disaster before leaving home for this sailing. He'd told her he dreaded this trip more than any other of his life. For Mrs. Hall, it was the Fourth of July itself that she dreaded, perhaps because of a similar tragedy just ten years earlier, when Capt. Hall had just missed being aboard another steamer that burned, drowning its captain's two children. Neither of the Halls had ever "rested easy" since that day.

THE KEEPER'S LIFE

Despite the relative isolation, the Cove Point Light assignment was desirable because the keeper's family could live with him—or her. From 1857 to 1859 the keeper was a woman, Sarah Thomas, who replaced her husband George upon his death. They lived on land, so they needed no boat for shopping, church, or other excursions. Nevertheless, it had its dark moments.

Friday, April 28, 1876 was as lovely a spring day as you could imagine on the Chesapeake. Charles Erdman, in his fourth year as keeper of the Cove Point Light, began his chores as usual, noting the temperature and wind direction for entry in his logbook. Whether he suddenly saw it or was alerted by a sickening odor carried on the breeze, he knew immediately this would not be a good day. The receding tide was bidding farewell to the badly decomposed body of a man washed up on the beach near the lighthouse compound. Finding nothing else to aid in its identification, Erdman painstakingly noted every item of clothing for a notice in the *Baltimore Sun*, before burying the body above the high-water mark:

> *dressed in a sailor's suit, with Sylvester hat, navy blue pants, oil overhauls, heavy yarn shirt and woollen plaid shirt, with black, blue and purple stripes, cassimer vest, gray and black stripes, and Eastern made boots. His height was five feet, eight inches, with boots and cap on, light hair, complexion fair, and weight 130 or 140 pounds.*

Just four years later, for the second time in his eight-year tenure at Cove Point, Erdman made another grizzly discovery on the beach. This time neither the victim's occupation nor the activity leading to his death was discernible. Erdman reported to *The Sun* that he had found the body of a drowned white man on the beach, south of the light:

> *The buzzards had eaten all the flesh off the head. The body looked to be 5 1/2 feet high, fair complexion and weight 145 pounds; had a shirt and pants on, with legs torn off; also a belt and knife. Most of the front upper teeth were out. Had on the left wrist what looked to be an American eagle and shield in India ink.*

Erdman also buried this body in the sand.

REAL HAPPINESS

Richard Daniels, a forty-year veteran with the lighthouse service, couldn't believe his eyes on the morning of July 28, 1913, as he counted ten barges off Cove Point, stretching out about a mile behind the tug *Augustine* (perhaps better named *Hercules*). Bound for Baltimore from Norfolk, it was the longest tow behind a single tug ever seen on the Chesapeake, and that made it shipping news in the *Sun*.

In 1915, as he celebrated his seventy-first birthday, Daniels compared his almost a decade as keeper of the Cove Point Light with his nephew's post as President Woodrow Wilson's secretary of the Navy. He surmised that he was having "more real happiness being the ruler of Cove Point and its fine lighthouse" than his nephew "runs up against any old time."

The secretary was known to call on his uncle at the lighthouse from time to time in the auxiliary yacht, *Dolphin*. Daniels returned the visits when he went to Washington. *The Washington Post* carried a light-hearted account of one of the older man's visits to his high-ranking nephew's home. The paper reported that after a warm welcome from the secretary, beginning with an invitation to enjoy cigars together on the back porch, the lighthouse keeper was treated to a carriage tour of Washington's sights. After noting that the septuagenarian "had reached manhood when times in the South were at their worst," the article ended with his account of the D.C. visit upon returning to Calvert County:

> *And do you know, the whole time I spent*
> *in Washington, the only person I saw*
> *trying to put on airs was that colored man*
> *who drove the carriage.*

Less than two years later, Daniels died suddenly of a heart attack while talking with the captain of the lighthouse tender *Maple*.

NOT A DESK JOB

Assistant keeper Paul Gray was on high alert on the night of September 22, 1924 due to gale-force winds whipping across the Bay, whistling in tiny crevices all around the beacon. By midnight, he had seen nothing unusual in the white caps reaching as far as he could see, when suddenly a small boat appeared, mercilessly tossed about by the waves, several hundred yards offshore. Hearing no sound of an engine, Gray knew the pleasure boat, about twenty-five feet long, was in trouble. He ran from the tower and dragged the station's rowboat 100 or so feet to the surf on the leeward side of the Point. Rowing out to the disabled boat, he discovered its captain was incapacitated, injured from being tossed about while trying to restart the engine. In desperation, the captain had thrown the anchor overboard, where the powerful force of the waves was now dragging it past the Point, while the boat started to take on water. Gray threw the captain a line to tow the cruiser back toward the lighthouse. But the gale was too strong, blowing both boats three miles off course, south of the beacon. Gray struggled against it for three hours. Shortly before dawn, they made it. The cruiser was tied up at the station, and the captain was given first aid. He would resume his attempt to reach Florida by the inland route as soon as he was able, and his boat, which had filled with water off the beach, was raised. Gray, according to the front page news report, "was none the worse for his experience, and was on duty at the station" the same day.

In the summer of 1933, the lighthouse crew had just enough warning on August 23 to make major decisions, such as whether to evacuate family members, as a fifty-five miles-per-hour gale advanced northward in the Chesapeake at dawn. The lighthouse would suffer considerable damage, necessitating a log entry three times longer than usual to describe the aftermath. Lighthouse keeper Horace Groom reported havoc wreaked on the buildings and grounds, flooded under two to three feet of water. Four shade trees were uprooted, two windows blown out in the powerhouse, and the electric plant knocked out of commission. And all the way up the road from the lighthouse grounds, the entire Point was flooded, deep enough to warrant rowboats to reach high ground.

It was an exceptional life, with some special moments, as when the keeper reported to the Maritime Exchange in October 1930, that an exhausted carrier pigeon, white and brown, had dropped at the lighthouse and was being cared for. It happened more than once. Three years later, assistant keeper Herman Metivier reported that he was extending the facility's hospitality to another fatigued carrier pigeon that had landed at the lighthouse. He placed notices in the newspapers in search of its owner.

One complaint (if it could be called that) may have been that maintaining the acreage around the light was more work than if it had been offshore, situated on a rocky outpost. Another may have been the reason given by first assistant keeper Lewis Cass Hook who, in 1887, resigned the post after less than a year, at first citing his health, but later telling the *Baltimore Sun* that the salary was too small.

3

THE COVE

*From slave-holding plantations
to a cluster of summer cottages,
a fisherman's paradise emerges.*

In stark contrast to the perils offshore of Cove Point, the waters in the cove could be a tranquil haven, with no more than a gentle rippling on its blue surface. In the shape of a crescent moon facing southeast on the Bay, the hollow between the north and south cusps of the cove on most days offered serenity to mariners seeking respite from the northeasterly winds that swept and sometimes pounded the north side of the Point, eroding the shoreline, while the beach within the cove's outstretched arms was curiously accreting.

Besides the lighthouse at its tip and the steamship wharf at the south end of the cove, there wasn't much else of special interest near the end of the bumpy road to Cove Point in 1828. To the north, there were the large, fresh water ponds fed by streams running through the forests on the highlands above them. To the south, large, wooded tracts of land, some of them farmed, and the wharf where the farmers brought their crops and picked up supplies offloaded from steamers making rounds on the Bay between Baltimore and Norfolk. Until 1864, when slavery was outlawed in Maryland, the cargo was likely loaded and unloaded by slaves. Between the mid-1700s and the Civil War, more than thirty percent of Maryland's population was Black, and most were slaves. Although Maryland did not secede from the Union, there was considerable pro-slavery sentiment, as the tobacco economy of the southern plantation areas, including Calvert County, relied on cheap labor.

Since the area was so rural, steamers likely stopped only when flagged by the manager, who also served as postmaster. After a damaging hurricane in October 1878, the wharf was out of commission until rebuilt. It was again taken down by a fire in 1892. The fire was reportedly started by some fishermen who used the warehouse at the end of the wharf, which had considerable freight inside, to warm up. They had spread sand on the warehouse floor and then built a fire on it, neglecting to extinguish it when they left. Until the wharf was rebuilt, the Weems Steamboat Company used a small boat to transfer passengers and mail from its steamship to shore. By 1907, it was generating more than $1,000 a year in freight (about $30,000 in 2020 dollars), and over $700 in passenger revenue (about $20,000 in today's currency).

The traffic sometimes resulted in accidents. In December 1913, a schooner owned by Solomons waterman and store owner J. F. Webster was at anchor with a cargo of 750 bushels of oysters aboard when it was rammed by the steamer *Anne Arundel*, backing out from the wharf. The Maryland,

Delaware and Virginia Railway Company, owners of the steamer, paid the claim and waived any right to the vessel.

Steamships were not only a gateway to markets for farmers' produce but also an opportunity for families to shop Baltimore's waterfront stalls and stores for items needed back home. For some, the steamers were a means of escape from the routines of rural life for a bit of excitement in the big city. That's what brought young Tom Buckler to the wharf on a warm Tuesday morning in August 1909. Tall and lanky, with auburn hair and grey eyes, he'd just turned twenty-one and was still living at home with his widowed mother and older brother. Unlike several of their neighbors on Cove Point Road who worked the Bay as oystermen, the two young men toiled in the nearby sawmill, where the pay was not bad but the work tedious and the days long. Tom was ready for some fun when he boarded the steamer *Westmoreland* for the run to Baltimore, a city whose attractions he planned to explore fully over the next three days. Not knowing what temptations he might encounter, he'd stuffed a pants pocket with all of his savings. The adventure, however, turned out far differently from anything he'd ever dreamed. As soon as he landed, the country lad was greeted by a stranger who called him "Cousin George," and said he'd been waiting for him since sun-up. "Welcome to our city!" the man bellowed, extending his arms as if expecting a hug. Tom stood back and quickly proclaimed the man's error. But the greeter was so friendly that the two finally left the wharf arm-in-arm.

A few hours of eating and drinking later, the camaraderie ended abruptly in a saloon, when the younger man felt his new friend's hand in his pocket. A chase ensued, the police joined in, and the greeter was arrested with $5 of Tom's money in his trousers, far less than the $16 (over $400 in today's currency) the lad claimed had been stolen from him. It was enough, however, for Tom's steamer ticket back to Cove Point the same afternoon. The *Baltimore Sun* headline the next day must certainly have added to his embarrassment: "'Cousin George' Loses $16: Thomas E. Buckler of Cove Point Goes Home, Sadder and Wiser."

It wasn't until 1908 that a schoolhouse was built (for White children) on the west side of Little Cove Point Road, a few hundred yards from its cutaway off Cove Point Road. Total annual enrollment for the '08-'09 school year was forty-one, with average attendance of twenty-two. Attendance was so erratic over the next sixteen years that state requirements forced the school's closure in 1928, despite the protests of parents. The students were thereafter bused to Solomons Elementary and the school building and one-acre lot sold. (It still stands today as part of a residence.) A school "for colored children" opened near Cove Point in 1914, also in the area of Little Cove Point Road. Total enrollment that first year was twenty-six, with an average attendance of twenty. School board records lack the kind of specifics recorded for the White school, such as the name of the first teacher, why the school was closed in 1930, or where the students were transferred.

A NEW PERSPECTIVE

By 1915, most mentions of Cove Point in Washington and Baltimore newspapers had started to reflect news other than tragic seafaring. The area was suddenly the epicenter of an unquenchable thirst on the part of the prospering urban populations for news relating to—of all things—sport fishing! An eight-column feature in *The Sun* said it all: "CHESAPEAKE BAY, THE GREAT NATIONAL FISHING GROUND." Under that headline, a successful fisherman was pictured adding to an overflowing bushel of trout, reportedly the "Result of One Hour's Catch with Line and Reel." The mouth of the Patuxent River near Cove Point was becoming the playground for Washington fishermen since the completion of the state roads leading from D.C. The reporter's enthusiasm for the sport was almost palpable:

> *When a fisherman gets either a rock or tailor (bluefish) on his hook he has to land the gamest fish which swims in Chesapeake waters. The excitement comes when the aquatic wiggler reaches the surface of the water, its body is bent in a half circle and its tail turned in*

*hook shape as though it is trying to cling
on, as the water is felt slipping from it.
Then look out for that last lunge which
sometimes sets it free, but often snaps
line, etc., and the monster swims off with
hook and all. That is the time a fish looms
up like a mountain. The fisherman's
excitement runs off with his imagination
and when that fish gets away—'the Lord
only knows how large they grow in the
Chesapeake Bay.'*

By 1920, *The Sun* also carried a popular and long-running column, "Fisherman's Luck and Hunting Notes," tempting readers with tales of huge catches in the Bay. The Washington *Evening Star* soon followed with its own weekly "Rod and Stream" column.

As the '20s roared in, the newspapers were reporting weekly on the plentiful catch awaiting recreational fishermen in the area's waters, including many thrilling hauls off or near the Cove Point Light. They also began to focus on one of the necessities of the recreational outing: Where to stay. A *Baltimore Sun* article mentioned that "the shores of Chesapeake Bay offer around two dozen resorts that will prove entirely satisfying for the summer vacation." The report offered no names or specific sites, other than to mention that going into the region's "real old homes" owned by people "descended from the aristocrats of the original Colonies," one would still find "that subtle charm of the old time Maryland days," and even larger hotels practicing "this ideal of genuine hospitality." Having given this assurance, the article's focus turned to listing the best fishing grounds on both the Eastern and western shores, all "within easy reach by comfortable steamers." (A bridge across the Chesapeake from Annapolis to Kent Island would not be built until 1952.)

In northern Calvert County, Chesapeake Beach, about 30 miles north of Cove Point, had become the Washington area's resort on the Bay's western shore as early as 1900, when the first train arrived with eager beach goers after a one-hour Honeysuckle Route through rural Maryland. On September 19, 1905, *The Washington Post* announced that commencing the next day, "Special Fisherman's Daily Express leaves 8:30 a.m.; returns at 6 p.m. 50 cents round trip." Others came by steamers from Baltimore that docked off a mile-long pier. With hotels, bathhouses, casinos, a dance pavilion, and a roller coaster, there was plenty for even landlubbers to enjoy.

Under the headline "Chesapeake Beach Night Fishing Good," an article in *The Washington Post* not only raved about the "seaside" resort's swimming and fishing but also noted that Ralph Garren's jazz orchestra was "furnishing snappy music for free dancing at the casino, the big restaurant on shore overlooking the bay."

"All of the amusements, including the big derby racer, are running full blast," the report exclaimed, and it was all "picturesquely situated, along with the boardwalk, over the water."

But the beach's boom crashed after the stock market plummeted and the Great Depression gripped the country. The posh resort lost its glamour, and by 1935, even the railroad stopped coming.

Adjacent to Chesapeake Beach, the small town of North Beach (originally North Chesapeake Beach) was also platted at the turn of the century, with vacation cottages laid out along some seven blocks of waterfront. Unlike its glitzy next-door neighbor, North Beach focused exclusively on fishing (by both summer vacationers and working watermen) and swimming in the waters that ads for both resorts described as "salt" but which were actually brackish. In July 1929, the *Evening Star* was advertising Washington motor coach service to North Beach three times a day from the bus terminal at 9th Street and Pennsylvania Avenue NW, leaving at 9 a.m, 1:30 p.m. and shortly after 5 p.m. (stopping in five other towns along the way).

In January 1935, the *Baltimore Sun* reported on a proposed, almost $10 million Negro resort and subsistence homestead colony on 500 acres near the Dares Wharf, less than five miles east of Prince Frederick, and three miles south of Plum Point in Calvert County. The colony, designed by nationally known Black architect Albert Cassell, would include 113 cottages, farm dwellings, a dairy, and a rug factory, as well as a hotel and casino. Just two days later, the newspaper reported that the project had been rejected by the federal Public Works Administration. Calvert County citizens had vigorously objected, based largely on the proposed shoreline site, immediately adjoining one of the most popular beaches in the vicinity. But the paper added that locals had previously objected to such a colony anywhere in Calvert County. According to the *Sun*, the federal agency reportedly regarded the project as considerably "overreaching the bounds" of PWA policy.

500 YARDS OF BAYFRONT?
YOURS FOR $2,500

On November 9, 1924, a two-column display ad in *The Washington Post* classifieds hawked "Desirable Waterfront Properties For Profitable Investment," leading off with:

> *105 acres at Cove Point on the Chesapeake Bay... 1 mile from Cove Point Lighthouse, 500 yards fronting on Bay Shore, elevated above sea level, good spring water. Fine sites for dwellings; wonderful bathing shore. Small dwelling, small barn and storehouse now on property...Price $2,500. A wonderful value at this low price.*

The sellers were George W. Hagelin and his wife Sarah. The Hagelin family was connected with Cove Point back at least to the Civil War. In 1862, first mate Charles M. Hagelin was rescued along with the captain and most of the passengers aboard the schooner *Manokin*, carrying "guano and groceries" when it was struck by the Brazilian steamer *Paraense* off Thomas Point (about fifty-eight miles to the north).

Hagelin went on to serve as Cove Point Lighthouse keeper from 1862 to 1868. His eldest son, John Henry Hagelin, born September 12, 1838, served as his first assistant from 1864 to 1866, and Mary Hagelin succeeded the young man in that post from 1866 to 1867. A decade later, a tragic accident brought John Henry home to the cove, when the brig *Chattanooga*, out of Baltimore, attempted to reach the mouth of the Patuxent River in a heavy snow squall. The ship, its "wheel chains having parted," became unmanageable and went aground on the Little Cove Point Bar. The next morning, struggling to get ashore, the captain, second mate Hagelin and a yeoman were drowned. The *Calvert Journal* reported:

> *By coincidence his body came ashore near the residence of his father Capt. Charles M. Hagelin, an old and respected citizen of this county. It is said the son had not been home for six years.*

Another Hagelin appeared in the *Baltimore Sun* more than a quarter of a century later under an eye-catching headline:

THINKS SON, 17, ELOPED...
ASKS POLICE TO HELP FIND HIM
—IN LOVE WITH HOUSEKEEPER.

The city and county police have been asked to find Robert M. Hagelin, 17 years old, of Cove Point, Calvert County, Md., son of Charles C. Hagelin, who disappeared from his home on February 3, and is thought to have eloped with Miss Dora Herschner, formerly of Catonsville, and until recently housekeeper for his father.

The senior Hagelin described his son as wearing a grey suit the last time the red-haired, blue-eyed teen was seen. Besides notifying the Baltimore Police Department, Hagelin went to Ellicott City, where he determined that no marriage license had been issued to the couple. Going next to the Herschner family home in Catonsville, he was told by the young woman's father that the couple had not made an appearance there.

Charles Hagelin told the newspaper that his first wife had died and his second wife had left him. He said he had kept house with his two boys until about four months earlier, when he secured the services of Miss Herschner as a housekeeper:

A love affair, he said, sprang up between Miss Herschner and his eldest son, and he notified Miss Herschner that her services were no longer required. Miss Herschner went to the home of her sister at Cove Point and later left for Baltimore. About a week later young Hagelin disappeared, and the father is of the opinion that they ran away and were married. He said that they could not have gone far, as his son had only $15 in cash when he left home.

But old man Hagelin was no match for young love. A few weeks later, the *Democratic Advocate*, a weekly newspaper in Westminster, Maryland, about 35 miles northwest of Baltimore, announced that a marriage license had indeed been issued to Robert and Dorothy. Eventually, the couple and their growing family moved to Egg Harbor, New Jersey, where Robert, by 1940 the father of six children, worked as a carpenter, and ministered to a nearby Christian congregation.

It was George W. Hagelin who owned much of the land around Cove Point in the 1930s. He also managed the steamboat wharf in the cove during the early 1920s and later served as postmaster for Cove Point—while operating a general store (of which the post office was a part) on Cove Point Road, just up the hill from the beach. According to his obituary in 1963, Hagelin, eighty-five, had also been a carrier for *The Washington Post* from 1950, walking the four-mile route every day until he retired, just four years earlier. The paper reported that he was survived by fourteen children (six sons/ eight daughters), more than seventy grandchildren and twelve great-grandchildren.

THE COVE POINT CLUB

Back in the 1920s, a few months after George W. Hagelin's real estate ad appeared in *The Washington Post* offering the "wonderful value" of Cove Point land, the *Evening Star* ran an intriguing article with a Baltimore dateline under the headline: "Cove Point Site Chosen for New Summer Resort:"

> *A group of New York businessmen, it is reported in real estate circles, have purchased a large tract of land at Cove Point, and will shortly begin construction of a Summer resort.*

The article mentioned that the site was close to Baltimore (60 miles), as well as Washington, and reachable by either train (presumably to Chesapeake Beach, but not beyond), boat or motor "in a short time." The names of the venture's interested parties were "kept secret," the article teased, adding that "by next week work of erecting bungalows and the boardwalk will be started," pursuant to plans said to be "of large nature."

The truth of the matter was that the property had been purchased by a group of Fairfax County, Virginia, investors. On April 30, 1925, the "Cove Point Club" had been incorporated in the State of Delaware by five prominent residents of Falls Church, Virginia. One of them was Wilbur Hinman, whose three-column obituary in *The Washington Post* some thirty-five years later described the eighty-eight-year-old Cleveland native as a "retired administrative assistant in the Farm Credit Administration and a member of the White House staff under four Presidents" (Theodore Roosevelt, Taft, Coolidge and Hoover). He'd also been "the first deputy clerk of the short-lived Commerce Court" and worked in the Department of Justice, the Internal Revenue Service and the Civil Service Commission. The other investors included a woman frequently mentioned in the *Post's* society column; a past postmaster and president of the East Falls Church Citizens Association; a business owner; and an executive of the American Legion post.

According to its articles of incorporation, the primary purpose of the new entity was to "conduct a club for recreation purposes, chiefly, for vacation and outing purposes." This plan was carried out over the next four decades through the rental of a number of summer beach cottages south of the county road leading to the site of the Cove Point Wharf. (A decade after the club's dissolution in 1962, the area would be developed as Cove of Calvert, a residential community between the Bay and Cove Point Road, southwest of Cove Point Beach.)

None of the incorporators served as officers of the new corporation. According to the Club's first annual report, this group included a scientist with the National Bureau of Standards and a government and industrial physicist. Later officers during the Club's thirty-seven-year history would include a mechanical engineer with the Bureau of Standards and Diamond Ordnance Fuze Laboratories, and a woman, Hope Peters, who had been one of the first yeomanettes to serve in the Navy in World War I, and had stayed on as a civilian until retiring in the late 1940s.

The Cove Point Club's arrival in 1925 signaled a change in the quiet cove. Suddenly, federal bureaucrats, scientists, engineers and other new faces were coming and going in the summer months, many of them drawn by the lure of the fantastic fishing touted weekly in D.C.'s daily press.

But a long-time Calvert County man had also had his eye on the cove and its wooded, undeveloped waterfront for the past two decades. In 1913, Maryland state Senator J. Cook Webster had purchased his first parcel of land there, a large tract that had been part of colonial Eltonhead Manor. In 1926 he added a two-acre parcel secured from the U.S. Government at public auction of excess lighthouse property. Finally in 1931, he bought the last fifty acres of property in the cove—enough to fulfill his own meticulous plans for a summer beach colony for Washington bureaucrats. The seller, as in the transfer to the Cove Point Club in 1925, was George W. Hagelin, who was still a major landowner in Cove Point.

A VERY DIFFERENT VISION

Over the years, Cook Webster had molded far bigger plans for the cove than the Fairfax investors. By 1930, automobile outings were growing in popularity, a trend unfortunately evidenced by the number of road accidents. (In Maryland alone, 132 persons were killed in auto accidents during the first five months of 1929, an increase of sixteen over the same period the previous year.) Decades before air conditioning would cool down either the government buildings or its employees' homes, Washington's workforce was looking farther down the Bay's western shore for summer cottage sites. To this Calvert entrepreneur, the time was right. His only child, Sarah Catherine Webster, an alumna of Syracuse University, with graduate credits from Johns Hopkins, had been married to World War I veteran William Bedford Glascock since 1928. Webster's business interests were prospering, and he had recently finished a two-year term as Maryland state senator (1931-33). By 1936, the real estate and financial markets were on the rebound, and all relevant indicators appeared favorable for the fulfillment of his vision—the dream of his adult life.

4

THE CUNNING OF J. COOK WEBSTER

The Greatest Thrill of Your Life

Best known by his middle name, Joseph Cook Webster lived all but his first seventeen years in Solomons, Maryland. He was born in 1873 to Silas and Linda Kelly Webster on Deal's Island, in Somerset County, between Taylor's Island and Crisfield on the Bay's Eastern Shore. (The town name later became Deal Island.) His father, like the hundreds of Websters born on the island over the next two-plus centuries, descended from John Webster, who'd arrived from Cornwall, England, in the mid-1700s, and had four sons, William, Meshack, Jebez and John. Their progeny are memorialized on the island by hundreds of Webster tombstones dating back to the eighteenth century in the graveyards at St. Paul's and Rock Creek United Methodist churches.

Cook Webster's love for the Bay and all its bounty came naturally in this small, watermen's community, which then, as now, hosted a fleet of skipjacks engaged in commercial oystering. As much as he enjoyed those shellfish, young Webster had no interest in making his livelihood as an oysterman. And although fishing would always be a favorite pastime, it was not at the top of his list either. The Bay's waters may have coursed through his veins and its winds through his lungs, but his head was filled with much bigger dreams.

At seventeen, like many others who'd left Deal's to seek their fortunes up or down the Bay, Cook sailed away to join his brother, John Fletcher Webster, who was operating a general merchandise store across the Bay in Solomons, near the mouth of the Patuxent River. The two-story operation, across the street from its own wharf on the Narrows in Back Creek, sold provisions to both homeowners and the busy flow of marine traffic. It was also a gathering place for local watermen after their day's work, luring them around its potbellied stove for story telling and peanut eating until the floorboards were covered with shells and it was time to retire for the night.

Cook married Sarah Elizabeth Saunders in 1899, and they had one child, Sarah Catherine, born in 1902. He worked in the store with his brother until buying him out in 1924. Later he brought two nephews into partnership, freeing himself up for his many other interests. As booming as it was, even Solomons' busiest store wasn't enough to satisfy his hunger for new enterprises.

Over three-plus decades beginning in 1901, Webster planted oyster beds in the Patuxent (starting right in front of his home on Solomons' Patuxent Avenue); formed the Patuxent Fish and Oil Company (1912) with three other prominent Solomons men;

and became a prominent charter boat captain frequently mentioned in the fishing columns of *The Washington Post* and the *Evening Star.*

Webster won election to the Maryland State Senate in 1930, the first Democrat to do so in many years. He would go on to incorporate the Solomons Island Yacht Club, serve as president of a Solomons bank, and acquire more than 4,000 acres of land in Calvert County. Among them were tracts traced back to the historic "Eltonhead Manor" (sometimes erroneously cited as "Elkton Head Manor") stretching north along the western shore of the Bay from the mouth of the Patuxent River to beyond Cove Point. And that wasn't all.

The few anecdotes about Webster passed down through the years suggest nothing of his business savvy, political skill, or extraordinary vision. On the contrary, without the historic record, we're left with a caricature of a man who is impatient to the point of irrational and reckless to the brink of manslaughter. Hulbert Footner, a prolific writer who settled near Solomons in the early 1900s, described Webster colorfully in one of his books:

> *On the island itself, the man I liked best was Cook Webster, the storekeeper, a smallish fellow of a dry leathery aspect, whose age is impossible to guess...He was always dressed in a full suit of store clothes and a derby hat. He loved to drive*

a sharp bargain, and was gleeful when he succeeded in overreaching you. The prices in his store were all but confiscatory...On the other hand, he had the kindest heart in the world; in times of stress on the island, he 'carried' the entire village, until the oystering or tourist trade looked up again. For this reason, nobody has ever been able to compete successfully with his store. (Charles' Gift, 1939.)

Portrait of Webster. (Courtesy Sarabeth Smith and Calvert Marine Museum)

Footner goes on to describe Webster as always having a cigar in his mouth, unsmoked, which would be flung to the ground "in a rage" when he lost his temper. Sometimes Webster's explosions were absurd, as when his boat motor failed to start for a duck hunting expedition one winter morning. "Snatching up his gun," according to Footner, while not claiming eyewitness of the scene, Webster "shot the engine." Another story describes Webster as a reckless driver clipping and knocking over a traffic officer's kiosk at an intersection in Baltimore, then driving away before the policeman could extricate himself. Again, a colorful if unauthenticated portrait.

THE DREAM

Cook Webster studied the plat he'd rolled out on his dining room table with obvious satisfaction. Much more than a mere map, it delineated the first section of the most ambitious project the shrewd entrepreneur had conceived in all his years as a shopkeeper, waterman, land speculator, Maryland state senator, and more. On it were the blocks, the lots, and the roads, including all the survey measurements, forming the first phase of his dream. It would be an exclusive, residential summer colony named for its location on an exquisite cove facing southeast on the Chesapeake Bay—Cove Point Beach. The first three of what would ultimately be nine, up to a quarter-mile long, bank-run gravel roads were laid out in straight lines running southeasterly from virgin wetlands to the shores of the Bay. Their names would reflect the lifestyle Webster envisioned for his new community—Park, Beach and Chesapeake drives. The fourth, the only memorial he fashioned for himself in the entire scheme, would be Webster Drive.

OPENING DAY

The lighthouse log entry for Saturday, April 18, 1936, was, as usual, meticulous and succinct. Keeper Horace Groom reported a "fresh breeze" from the northwest in the morning, remaining light from the north in the afternoon, with a temperature of sixty degrees. The day's work was to clean up the grounds.

(U. S. National Archives)

True to his orders, Groom stuck to the formulaic entries of the past 108 years, reporting nothing of the commotion a few hundred yards down the road where real estate agents handpicked by the county's most influential citizen were showing wooded lots on the Bay to prospective buyers—federal government bureaucrats, mainly, but others as well. They'd been lured the sixty miles from Washington by quarter-page ads and breathless articles in both *The Washington Post* and *Evening Star*, some heralding the opening of Cove Point Beach as "the greatest

success in all Washington beach property history."
All this before the first lot was sold.

To its founder, every word was true. Others would
snicker at the hype. "Atlantic City of the South!" *Well,
not really.* The Jersey Shore resort, with its 1,200 or
more hotels, boardwalk, oceanfront beach, and much
more, had been the "go to" vacation destination of

well-to-do Washingtonians for decades. The ads were taking a page from the Atlantic City playbook, which called that resort "Baghdad by the Sea." Webster's subsequent ads similarly spared no hyperbole. "No sea nettles!" *Are you kidding?* But when the window dressing was blown away, two truths remained: The Cove Point Beach development embraced the most beautiful white sand beach on the Bay; and off its shores was indeed the best fishing. As one ad promised, there truly was a thrill awaiting visitors who might be seeing the fulfillment of their own dreams:

> *For many years, hundreds of people who have fished off this BEAUTIFUL POINT, with the great government lighthouse and broadcasting station, have asked why they could not own a summer home here—WHY this delightful spot had not been developed, as it has absolutely the FINEST BEACH, the MOST BEAUTIFUL TREES, and the MOST MAGNIFICENT SCENERY of any place on the GREAT CHESAPEAKE BAY!*

"Drive down today," the ad urged, "bring the whole family," and "GET THE GREATEST THRILL OF YOUR LIFE!"

A more serene, tri-fold brochure with pictures of the first cottages, the roads and the 200-foot pier, whispered a softer, and more accurate, enticement, "A Perfect Setting for a Restful Summer."

The Opening Day 1936 ads, as large as a quarter-page in *The Washington Post* and its rival *Evening Star,* revealed the vision of a man accustomed to baiting the hooks that landed the biggest fish. The catch Cook Webster was luring now was federal employees toiling in the halls of the nation's capital and pocketing enough savings to buy a vacation home some sixty miles away. "Three miles of sandy beach," "200 foot fishing pier" (until washed away a decade or so later),"paved roads," "finest salt water bathing," "finest fishing," "largest lots of any nearby resort," and "financing available" were some of the lures.

A year later, there would be an added enticement, as reported in *The Washington Post* under the headline "Electricity Is Installed at Cove Point Beach," an improvement said to indicate the return of prosperity after the Depression. Many of the homes in nearby Solomons Island, nine miles to the south and the most famous community at this end of the narrow Calvert peninsula, lacked electricity, even in the early 1940s, not to mention indoor plumbing.

To manage all this, from the surveys, layouts, and permits all the way through advertising in *The Washington Post* and the *Evening Star*, to property sales, Webster hired the area's top real estate developer, Leon Ackerman, and his associate, a real estate agent. Ackerman recently had developed Long Beach, a small, unpretentious, summer home community twelve miles north, and would go on to become one of the area's biggest developers, specializing in waterfront resorts and homesites.

The handwritten contract between Webster and the two men, dated the sixth day of April, 1936, went on for almost six pages, spelling out in detail his expectations for the "development and marketing" of a large tract of land known as the Cove Point Beach property. Specifically, the developers, in return for fifty percent of the purchase price of each lot sold, were to survey the property; clear and properly prepare the development for sale; and construct each year during the contract term not less than 7,500 feet of gravel roadway. They would also "properly advertise" and maintain one or more salesmen on the property at all times from May through September.

The contract listed the sales prices for all lots covered by the agreement. The $495 price tag for waterfront lots was reduced in each parallel zone as the lots fell away from the Bay and closer to the wetlands on the north side of the property. A few large lots (100 x 200 feet) along the wetlands were to be offered for as little as $95.

RACIAL EXCLUSION

Webster reserved to himself the right to withhold approval of any contract negotiated by the developers, specifically adding a covenant requiring his approval of each and every buyer during the first half-dozen years of sales. If, however, the contract complied with the price schedule as well as the required ratio of one waterfront to three others, Webster would pay the developers twenty-five percent of the contract price, so long as the proposed buyer was not "of the negro race." His exclusion of African Americans from initial sales of properties in the new community was crystal clear, and Webster wanted to make it perpetual by including another covenant in every deed specifying that "no part or portion of the said land or buildings thereon shall ever be rented, leased, sold, transferred, conveyed or otherwise vested in or in trust for any person other than one of the white or Caucasian Race." Exceptions were noted for transfers by will, inheritance, or court-ordered sale.

Racial restrictive covenants such as Webster's appeared in the late nineteenth century, prohibiting future sales to minority groups, usually Blacks, but depending on the part of the country, also Jews, Chinese, Japanese, Mexicans, or any non-Caucasians. In the early 1920s, such covenants occurred nationally as the North and Midwest picked up and extended the practice, primarily in cities, largely in response to the rapid urbanization of immigrants and migrants of color, whether from the rural South or abroad.

As a form of private contract, these covenants were legally enforceable in court under a 1926 District of Columbia Court of Appeals decision upheld by the U.S. Supreme Court. The court said that members of the excluded class could similarly refuse to sell their own property, and thus there was no discrimination within the civil rights clauses of the Constitution.

That ruling held until the Supreme Court in 1948 declared racially discriminatory covenants unenforceable by the courts. Maryland lawyer (and future U.S. Supreme Court Justice) Thurgood Marshall was one of the attorneys who successfully argued the case.

It would be twenty years before the Fair Housing Act, part of the Civil Rights Act of 1968, made it unlawful for a landlord to discriminate against or prefer a potential tenant based on their race, color, religion, or national origin, when advertising or negotiating the sale or rental of housing. Gender discrimination was added to the prohibitions in 1974.

The second phase of Cook Webster's dream was platted a few months later, in November 1936. It added two more north-to-south gravel roads (Holly and Cedar) and the continuation of Calvert Boulevard. While Lighthouse Boulevard, running about seven-tenths of a mile from the community's entrance to the lighthouse at Cove Point, was the resort's main artery, Calvert would be its *vena cava*, the only other road running parallel through most of the development.

THE ROAD COVENANT

One of the most important covenants in every original deed described a road maintenance fee, necessary because all of the roads, with the exception of Lighthouse Boulevard (which the Websters deeded to Calvert County in 1947), were intended to remain privately owned by the Websters, their heirs or assigns, in perpetuity. To assure that funds would always be available "for the construction, reconstruction and maintenance of the streets in the subdivision," the purchaser agreed for themselves and whomever followed them in ownership to pay a fee by June 1 of each year. To avoid any future debate—and certainly any argument or legal hassle (he thought) over how much that fee would be in future years, Webster adopted the same inflation-based formula ("a sum equal to $5.00") recently used by Ackerman in the deeds to lots in Long Beach. Decades later, it would take a ruling by Maryland's highest court to confirm that this was a stroke of genius rather than a monumental error.

The other covenants in the deeds were more common to those of most residential developments, including the exclusion of "poultry, hogs, and other domestic animals" from the waterfront resort.

COME ON DOWN!

Webster's reputation as a sportsman undoubtedly contributed to southern Calvert's draw as an attractive recreation site for Washingtonians. Long before he laid out his plans for a summer resort colony, his name had appeared frequently in the weekly fishing columns of the Washington press. In early June 1931, Perry Miller's "Rod and Stream" column in the *Evening Star* reported that in one day's trolling off Point Patience in the Patuxent River, State Senator J.C. Webster of Solomons and his nephew (Preston Webster of Baltimore) had landed eleven rockfish, weighing from four to six pounds, and a trout tipping the scales at four and a half pounds.

Miller later reported that some 40,000 anglers were believed to have fished from Solomons (the takeoff point for fishing near Cove Point) during the 1935 season, half of them coming from the nation's capital and vicinity. One captain, Harry Woodburn, was planning on luring schools of bluefish to the Cove Point Bar by throwing bushels of ground alewives in the water when they first arrived. "If there is one thing these fish like," Miller reported, "it is to have their meals served to them in this fashion."

A later column reported that "State Senator J.C. Webster of Calvert County hauled in the first big rock of the fall season off Point Patience while trolling with a feather," his prize weighing in at the fifteen pound limit, followed by several other "big boys" averaging ten pounds. And Jack Hawley's "Out Fishin'" column in *The Washington Post* described Webster as "an old resident of Solomons," writing that he'd caught another fifteen-pounder along with eight rockfish averaging five pounds.

Photos such as the one in the *Evening Star*, May 2, 1936, showing more than thirty bluefish, each at least twenty-five inches long, strung together at a dock over the caption, "Blues caught in the Bay off Cove Point, Md., near the mouth of the Patuxent River," certainly added to the allure.

Fishermen could find rooms at Solomons for $1 a night, while meals ran about $1.50 a day, and four hours aboard a charter fishing boat with up to five sportsmen was $5. J.C. Webster was included on a list of four boat captains for whom the columnist would personally "vouch for their equipment and ability." (The other three were also well-known entrepreneurs, George Bowen, J.C. Lore, and Harry Woodburn.) The columnist urged calling ahead, citing station-to-station fees of only thirty cents.

Before and after the much heralded opening of the Cove Point Beach resort, *The Washington Post* would attract more attention to southern Calvert by lauding its harbor as "one of the best fishing spots within reasonable driving distance of Washington," although it also described the last twenty miles (south of Prince Frederick) as so twisting and turning that "you sometimes meet yourself coming back," and urged that the road be straightened. Apparently not much had changed in the route since 1922 when the *Post* ran AAA's road map under the headline "Drive to Solomon's Island Is at Its Best—Fishing Season at Its Height." Directions accompanying the map instructed "sharp turn to right at end of road... caution...Turn next left...avoid right-hand diagonal roads...Through irregular four-corners...avoid left hand road at store" and so on. (It wouldn't be until the 1980s with the completion of a divided state highway running from D.C. all the way to Solomons and beyond that the drive would be a straight shot down Route 4, without fear of a sudden slowdown behind a tractor coming off a field.)

Real estate pages, along with quarter-page ads for Cove Point Beach, ran articles reporting brisk sales of lots near the "best fishing grounds" within easy reach of Washington. The growing number of curious readers driving down to check it out was probably what prompted lighthouse keeper Groom to post "No Trespassing" signs at the north and south sides of the government's property. Just weeks after the new community's grand opening, the *Post* ran an article that couldn't have been more glowing if it had been written by Webster or Ackerman themselves (especially since the superlatives were drawn straight from the developers' ads). Under the headline "Many Lots Sold in Chesapeake Development—Cove Point Beach Attracts Many Washingtonians Seeking Homesites," the article reported:

> *Quite a number of lots have been sold at Cove Point Beach, new development on Chesapeake Bay. This beautiful point, with its Government lighthouse and broadcasting station, has been the mecca for fishermen. They have loved this spread of white sandy beach, the wide expanse of sea-green water and the beauty of this spot so endowed with all the good things of nature.*

The lavish praise continued:

> *Here is indeed the summer homeland for every true lover of summer sport. More than six miles of wide, white, sandy beach are here and more than 1,100 acres of beautifully wooded estates. It is one of the finest fishing grounds on Chesapeake Bay and a panoramic vista of natural beauty, where sky, forest and sea seem to blend in beautiful coloring.*

The article reported that "hundreds of families are taking advantage of the fine weather...to get their first glimpse of this delightful new subdivision."

But that was only part of it. The article also claimed that the developer had made it possible for every family in Washington to secure a summer estate in this lovely spot, at remarkably low prices.

Cook Webster would not live to see the last two plats formalized, in 1947 and then in 1956. Already in bad health toward the end of 1937, he executed a power of attorney on August 21, granting his wife Sarah Elizabeth authority to act on his behalf in all of his affairs. His death nine months later on May 17, 1938, ended a career more industrious—and diverse—than Calvert County would soon see again. His ingenuity in the planning and execution of his pinnacle project on the Chesapeake Bay—from his choice of developer to the extraordinary advertising campaign—would guarantee its success. And while the *Post's* report of "hundreds of families" motoring down to see the new resort in its first weeks may have been an exaggeration, many did come. Among them—a princess.

5

THE LEGEND
OF TRYN TRAVA

*A tale of princes and princesses, war and
survival, a mother's love, and a woman's resolve*

How Natalie Scheffer, "Princess Wolkonsky" in an
earlier life and far away place, learned about Cove
Point Beach is not known. It may have been from
Webster's ads. Or, her grandchildren say, friends in
Washington, D.C., exiles like her from Czarist Russia
who fled during or after the Bolshevist Revolution of
1917, may have told her about the newly opened,
unspoiled colony by the sea. It certainly fit the
description she had penned of the places she'd loved
in her native land—the countryside outside Moscow,
for example, where the young bride had settled with
her groom:

> *I reveled in the freedom, in the scent of the
> soil and of the lilacs that surrounded the
> garden in a thick circle. I rejoiced over every
> new sprout, every freshly opened flower...
> I loved with all my heart the immense spaces
> of the fields, with the whirling starling...and
> in the winter, the softness of the snow, the
> transparence of the air and the silence.*

And later, while fleeing the oncoming Red army as a single mother with two, very young boys, thinking always of their well-being:

> *When summer came I was in need of rest and wanted to provide the children with sea-baths and a sand-beach instead of the dust of the town.*

All this and more she found at Cove Point Beach in the spring of 1936, and within months became one of its first summer residents.

Who was Natalie Scheffer? The answer to that question is a fascinating twentieth century tale of princes and princesses, war and survival, a mother's love, and a woman's resolve. In a memoir published in 1930, Natalia Petrova (a nom de plume) described the life of comfort and privilege into which she'd been born in 1889, and the terrifying world that confronted her every turn after the Bolshevist revolution of 1917—two existences so different that she titled her memoir *Twice Born in Russia*. Independence, creativity and resourcefulness seemed to have come naturally in her earliest years, when in the absence of her siblings (an older sister and brother) or other playmates, she created a make-believe world with dolls beneath her father's writing table, imagining his boots to be the front door and his spurs the doorbell. The role-playing took a different turn when her sister, on holiday from boarding school, would suddenly proclaim herself a surgeon, and amputate Natalie's dolls' legs or cut open their stomachs, reducing the little one to bitter tears.

A child's-eye view of family life, centering around formal Sunday lunches for twenty to thirty relatives—and "governesses of all nationalities"—at the big, grey house of an austere grandmother, followed by a ballet lesson around the piano in the "dancing-room," gives insight into a world of privilege in the realm of the Russian aristocracy. As Natalie put it, "reality with all its experience was very far away from me."

Reality of one sort did intrude, however, when at seven she lost her father, the sudden victim of heart failure in the night. Surrounded by flowers and incense, his body lay in repose in the dining room for three days of visitation and services. Veils draped over every mirror in the home, in respect to the Russian superstition that a man who sees his reflection in a mirror in a house where there is a dead body, must die soon after, himself. Unable to believe he could actually be dead, Natalia finally slipped out of bed during the night and mounted the steps to peer into her father's coffin, "hoping he would wake up."

She lived with her mother—from whom her father had been estranged—until she, too, died, five years later. Then came boarding school. She became a "zealous follower" of the orthodox religion under the sway of a highly religious Russian language teacher, whom she emulated:

*In my desire to manifest my zeal, I began
to instruct my German maid in the orthodox
religion and did so with such obstinacy
and eloquence, that she disowned Protes-
tantism after six months. I spent all my
pocket-money buying sacred books, Lives
of Saints, and images.*

In later years, the images of saints—more specifically "icons"—would play a major role in her choice
of professions, as well as her new life in Cove Point
Beach. But before all that, she would marry a prince,
bear two sons, divorce, and endure ten tumultuous
years in Bolshevist, famine-torn Russia. There's
not a word in the memoir about what led to the
dissolution of her marriage, nor is her husband's
name (Prince Nicholas Wolkonsky, Chamberlain to
the court of Czar Nicholas II) ever mentioned. (In
her Introduction to the book, American author and
columnist Dorothy Thompson comments that "she
maintains an intense reserve about all the more
intimate phases of her life, commendable in a well-
mannered lady, but disappointing in literature.")
For seven years, despite clear evidence of her
willingness and ability as a single mother to work
hard to support her family, she remained on a list
of Russians "of non-proletarian origin," dismissed
by the regime as "dust and litter," "useless ballast,"
"alive only because 'all princes and their like' were
not hanged in time."

By the time she wrote her extraordinary account of those years, she had married journalist Paul Scheffer, Moscow correspondent for the German newspaper *Berliner Tageblatt*. His status as a distinguished (non-Russian) European afforded her some measure of protection, and ultimately, her ticket out of the Soviet Union. Along with her sons, the couple left Moscow in 1928, eventually emigrating to Washington, D.C., first via Paris, then New York. (Paul Scheffer reportedly was the first foreign journalist to be refused a re-entry permit into the Soviet Union in 1929 for his critical reporting.)

AN EXILE "COLONY"

The writing of a memoir about her life in pre-revolution Russia, and her family's survival through the following decade, must have been cathartic, for by 1934, as a resident of Washington, Natalie Scheffer was able to write about the experience in a very different vein. By this time, she was a key player in the Russian émigré "colony," as *The Washington Post* society pages called it. The newspaper's account ran under the headline "Russians Make a Play From Their Own Lives:"

> *Old Russia lives again in the heart of Washington. Out of a group of some 60 refugees, half of this number have set to work reliving the lives they had before coming to this country and reenacting the experiences that brought them here.*

The play, performed for the benefit of Washington's St. Nicholas Russian Orthodox Church, founded in 1930, centered around the title question "How Do You Like This Country?" The paper reported "the general attitude" of the characters, was "one of gratitude toward the Americans who have given home to the homeless," and even included touches of "sly humor."

In February 1935, Mrs. Paul Scheffer (married women were seldom referred to by their own given names) was reported working on the elaborate decorations for the masked ball at the Shoreham Hotel, to mark the last day before Lent. That year's theme was "Maslenitsa," the gayest festival on the old Russian calendar, and the motif would be Russian fairy tales, carried out in the decorations and costumes.

Later in the year, the newspaper reported that Mrs. Scheffer would be in charge of exhibits at the annual St. Nicholas Fair in Washington, held by the Circle of Thirty, "a group of Russians of the old regime," for the benefit of "the little orthodox church on Church Street and for educational purposes." The *Evening Star* called the organization the "Circle of Russians," adding to its purposes "the perpetuation of old Russian arts and crafts and to raise funds for cultural needs among Russian refugees."

Natalie's elder son, Prince Dimitri Wolkonsky, a dashing, dark-haired bachelor in his early twenties, starred in many of these events, as when he performed his "famous sabre dance" to the accompaniment of a stringed orchestra at the annual fair hosted by the St. Nicholas Club the same year.

(Courtesy Nicholas Wolkonsky)

The following March, both of the young princes (as they continued to be known in émigré circles) were featured in newspaper reports announcing the upcoming "White Ball" for the church's benefit. Prince Dimitri Wolkonsky and a lucky young lady were designated to lead the polonaise (a ceremonial, march-like dance) that opened the ball, while his brother, Prince Peter Wolkonsky, was assisting in the arrangements.

TRYN TRAVA

In mid-August of 1936, after just a few months of advertising their waterfront oasis, Cook Webster and his wife Sarah Elizabeth sold one of the first lots in Cove Point Beach to Natalie P. Scheffer. Toward the north (the wetlands) end of Beach Drive, the lot, from all appearances, was in the middle of nowhere, populated by wild berry bushes, hollies, towering pines and dwarf evergreens of enough varieties to keep a botanist busy for a week. And it was quiet. So quiet you could hear the whistle of the redwing blackbirds swooping over the nearby marsh, the rustle of a rabbit in a thicket, or the steps of a deer treading cautiously through the woods. It was a place reminiscent of the countryside that enveloped the first years of her marriage, where she had reveled in "the immense spaces of the fields, with the whirling starling." Within months, she had built a small cottage, and named it Tryn Trava, later explaining:

*According to Russian legend, it means
a flower which blooms only once in a
lifetime and then only on a special night.
In the Russian language and songs, Tryn
Trava assumed the meaning of "don't
worry." Both the legend and the meaning
of the word were most befitting the origin
and purpose of the place.*

The intriguing name was painted top center of the
front window trim along with the year 1937 framed
by shutters emblazoned with large daisies, much like
the clusters that would bloom in her front yard in the
spring alongside the coneflowers and Siberian iris.

(Courtesy Nicholas Wolkonsky)

On weekends and holidays in the winter, she could
again wake to "the softness of the snow, the trans-
parence of the air and the silence," just as she had in
her homeland decades earlier.

(Courtesy Nicholas Wolkonsky)

Another connection to a place and time long past were the visits of friends from far away—this time sixty or so miles when they came from Washington. But this cottage could not accommodate many overnight guests, as had her country house outside of Moscow before the revolution. So over the next two years, she purchased the two adjacent lots to the north. She later explained that these purchases enabled her to expand the cottage, as well as to build a "pavilion," a guesthouse for overnight visitors. Like her own cottage, it would seem like something from folklore.

The Princess's "pavillion" on Beach Drive, with the original dark wood siding and yellow shutters, in 2019. (Courtesy Carol Booker)

She explained later how the pavilion furthered the purpose of Tryn Trava:

> *During times of financial hardship, money was spent on a place where some could come to escape from the pressures of work, where others could come to find peace, and where all could come to join in mutual friendship and a common desire to live and work so that Tryn Trava would bloom as the legend said it would. Tryn Trava was a place where people from different walks of life, culture and beliefs would gather for a single purpose of enjoying the sun, the sand and the sea.*

There was something missing, however, given that most of the time spent at Cove Point was on weekends and holidays, and most of her visitors were, like Natalie and her sons, members of the Russian Orthodox Church. There were no such religious services in Calvert County.

"The need for spiritual guidance became a consuming desire for all of us," she explained, "and so, in 1940 we decided to build a chapel."

CHRIST AT THE SEA

Scheffer recruited the design services of Dimitri Birkin, a Russian émigré himself and an engineer with the Edward G. Budd Manufacturing Co., Philadelphia's largest. Several pages of drawings on his letterhead proposed a six-sided structure crowned by an onion shaped cupola (symbolizing a flame of prayer rising to the heavens) and a cross.

(Courtesy Calvert County Historical Society)

Once the plans were approved, Birkin worked through the summer with Scheffer, her two sons, and a local builder, Capt. John Lusby, who was also a property owner at Cove Point. When they'd finished, the chapel, according to her notes, "stood in its rightful place to the left of the main entrance of Tryn Trava." It was blessed the same year "in a colorful ceremony" by a visiting priest, one of several who would visit Tryn Trava over the years. The door of the chapel was always open, and services were held on Sundays and holidays. At other times, Scheffer would go there just "to rest and pray."

Woman at entrance to the Chapel. (Courtesy Nicholas Wolkonsky)

She named the chapel Christ at the Sea in memory of an ancient, small, wooden chapel near Moscow, *Spas na Boru* (Christ at the Woods), which had been destroyed along with other places of worship during the Revolution.

It soon became apparent that something else was missing. The Russian chapel required no organ (a choir sufficed), no elaborate altar (a simple table was used) or even seats (the congregation stood). What the chapel with its plain, freshly painted interior was lacking, in her words, was "the solemn atmosphere to which we all were accustomed."

Scheffer's youthful obsession with Russian religious art by this time had morphed into the profession of "iconographer," which she practiced as chief of the Slavic Division at Dumbarton Oaks Research Library and Collection in Washington, D.C.. Although she had never done it before, she knew what the chapel should look like:

> *Thus, one morning, while all were asleep, I went to the chapel and found a table and a ladder which had been used for painting the ceiling. With these in hand, and armed with a supply of charcoal, brushes and tempera paint, I began to paint murals.*

On the center wall she painted the "Deisus," the "most important composition as well as an absolute requirement of the Russian Orthodox Church."

Deisus Icon. (Courtesy Carol Booker)

It depicts Christ on the Throne with the Virgin Mary and Saint John the Baptist standing beside him. On the other walls she painted mural-size images of saints, most of whom represent family names, including St. Peter (for her younger son and her father), St. Dimitri Rostowski (her elder son), St. Nicholas, the Wonderworker (father of her sons), and Saint Natalie (her own saint's name).

The religious observances, holidays, and typically warm summer weekends over more than two decades after the chapel was built would see a steady flow of Russian visitors to Tryn Trava. Like Scheffer, several also bought lots, leading to stories many years later about the "Russian colony" in Cove Point, and, especially intriguing, the rumored existence of a Russian "safe-house" during the Cold War. Among the purchasers were former members of the White Russian Army who had fought against the Bolsheviks in the revolution. There was a former general, George Ivitsky, and a research analyst with the Department of the Interior, Nicholas de Gelon-Ichenzeff.

Another was Irene Mishtowt, once a Lady-in-Waiting to Czarina Alexandra, who was murdered along with the Czar and their children during the 1917 overthrow. The wife of Ilarion V. Mishtowt, the former naval attaché at the Russian embassy, Madame Mishtowt might have been inclined to play Tchaikovsky's Sixth Symphony on the phonograph for visitors at her Cove Point cottage. Pyotr Ilyich Tchaikovsky was, after all, her great uncle.

Serge Koushnareff was also a musician in an earlier life, reportedly a pupil of the great Rachmaninoff. A top official with the Bureau of Foreign Commerce, he turned a trained eye on the cargo ships sailing up and down the Bay as he and his wife Jessie walked the beach at their summer home in Cove Point.

Wsevolod and Serafine Joukowski also followed Scheffer to Cove Point. Serafine was secretary of the Russian Children's Welfare Society, founded in 1926 to help Russian children whose families fled after the start of the Bolshevik Revolution. Before that, she had assisted her husband in welfare work with Russia's Third Army.

YOUNG PRINCES AND PRINCESSES

In 1940, the same year she built the chapel, Natalie transferred ownership of an adjacent lot to her elder son, Dimitri, then twenty-six. He had married a talented and vivacious young woman, Lubov Doubiago, whose father had been a general in the White Russian army. She was known on the society pages as "Princess Wolkonsky," or occasionally, "Princess Lubov Wolkonsky." Together with his brother Peter and Capt. Lusby, Dimitri built a charming cottage on the property, which still stands today. Lubov, formerly a professional singer, joined her husband in numerous appearances at fundraisers for the church and other émigré causes, where she sang gypsy songs in Russian costume, accompanied by her husband on guitar.

Lubov Doubiago had come to the United States at twenty-two and remembered well what life was like before the revolution. All of that was forgotten on the weekends the couple spent at Cove Point, where Dimitri showed off his athletic skills with dives off the 200-foot community fishing pier (long since demolished in storms), while Lubov enjoyed surfcasting for blues and rockfish.

In 1939, the couple was included in a large *Washington Post* feature on the lives of some of the

Dimitri Wolkonsky diving off Cove Point pier; Lubov Wolkonsky ready to surfcast from beach. (Courtesy Nicholas Wolkonsky)

approximately 100 former Russian elites who'd forged new careers in the capital. Lubov's worst memory was of hiding in a cellar in Kiev "from the turmoil outside" while making her way through Crimea and Turkey to America. Her most "wistful" memory of Russia was not unlike the musings of her mother-in-law, as she nostalgically recalled childhood at her grandmother's country house, with its "fruit garden, flowers, berries, trees, vegetable garden," as though some enchanted place.

Her full-time job as a young wife was selling dresses in a downtown specialty store, while Dimitri was working in a photography studio. Both would eventually move onward and upward—she to a position with the Library of Congress, from which she would retire after twenty-five years as a senior research analyst. Dimitri became well known as a freelance photographer, whose credit line frequently appeared with fashion and society photos in *The Washington Post* and the *New York Times*.

In 1942, they celebrated the birth of a daughter whom they named Nathalie, in honor of the family's matriarch. Elizabeth ("Dee-Dee") followed in 1948, and Nicholas, in 1951.

Lubov holding Nathalie in front of the cottage on Beach Drive. (Courtesy Nicholas Wolkonsky)

Three generations worshipped in the little chapel of Christ at the Sea over two decades at Cove Point, albeit in two different locations. From its first site nestled among the pines at the end of Beach Drive, Natalie Scheffer moved the chapel in 1946 (with the help of her sons and Capt. Lusby) to a space she felt more befitting its name, that is, closer to the sea, beside a new cottage she built for herself on the corner of Chesapeake Drive and Lighthouse Boulevard. Unlike the original Tryn Trava, the new cottage was a simple, white, cinder block structure that her grandchildren believe she modeled after rural houses she'd admired on a trip to Mexico.

Nathalie Wolkonsky with her cousin Alex Doubiago at the Lighthouse. (Photo by Dimitri Wolkonsky. Courtesy Wolkonsky family)

Not all members of the third generation were as enthusiastic about devotions in the chapel as their grandmother would have liked. Nicholas, the youngest, remembers hiding in the woods when called to worship. His petite, soft-spoken grandmother, he recalls, insisted he and his sister kneel barelegged for what seemed like "hours" on the rough, sandy floor before the altar. He much preferred combing the beach for treasures, exploring under and over fallen trees near the cliffs, sometimes "scooping crabs" from the branches.

Nicholas and his sisters spent every summer at Cove Point until he was ten or twelve years old, in the care of a Russian nanny (about "five feet, two inches and built like a barrel—stocky but not fat") who spoke no English. She would ring a cowbell to summon the children to come home, and even cook an eel if Nicholas happened to catch one. Then, on Friday evenings, he would listen intently for the sound of the car bringing his mother to Cove Point. Since Lubov did not drive, two colleagues at the Library of Congress would drive her down for the weekend, sleeping in the cottage's attic bedroom. On Saturday, they were all off to Evans Pier in Solomons, sometimes stopping along the way for ice cream at the little store at the junction between Cove Point Road and the rural route down to the island, especially if Uncle Peter was along. (He loved to play the store's slot machines.)

Sadly, Dimitri and Lubov had separated when Nicholas was just three years old, and divorced a few years later. For years, the only memento of the prince remaining at the pink cottage was a black and white mural of the lighthouse, enlarged to a 37 x 52 inch poster from a photo taken by Dimitri, which he had mounted on the wallboard. To the youngsters, it was a remembrance of a very special time.

When the Wolkonsky cottage on Beach Drive was renovated in the 1990s, the mural was cut out of the wallboard and donated to the Calvert Marine Museum, where it resides today. (Courtesy Calvert Marine Museum)

DA SVIDANYA, COVE POINT

In 1966, Natalie Scheffer, then seventy-seven, was no longer physically able to travel to Tryn Trava from her northwest Washington, D.C. home. Many of the friends who had visited her in Cove Point over the years had died, moved away, or were also unable to travel. Her younger son, Peter, was overseas with the Army, in which he had served since World War II. Dimitri, since his divorce from Lubov, no longer came to Cove Point. Natalie sold the beach house, along with the chapel, "with the understanding that the chapel would not be destroyed or desecrated."

Her wish was honored. The new owners donated the chapel to the Calvert County Historical Society, and

The chapel at its current site in the historic village at Herrington Harbour North, in Anne Arundel County. (Courtesy Carol Booker)

a preservationist moved it to an historic homesite in Dunkirk. Around 2008, recognizing that the precious icons, as well as the deteriorating exterior, were in need of extensive repair, another preservationist moved the chapel to the historic village at Herrington Harbour North in Anne Arundel County. It stands there today under the auspices of the Deale Area Historical Society.

Natalie Scheffer's cottage on the northeast corner of Chesapeake Drive and Lighthouse Boulevard was eventually razed, making way for a modern home. "The legend of Tryn Trava came true," just as the princess wrote:

> *Tryn Trava bloomed only once in our lifetime, and while it bloomed we all forgot our worries.*

6

THE INVASION

Foxholes on the beach;
tear gas seeping into the house;
troops in the backyard—it felt like war!

The U.S. Army rolled onto Cove Point Beach in 1943 in tanks, jeeps and trucks disgorged from the gaping bows of amphibious assault ships. In about three hours, thousands of combat troops would be ashore, followed in less than twelve hours by all their supplies and vehicles.

Army Amphibious Landing Craft approaching Cove Point. (Courtesy U.S. National Archives)

The Army's invasion was no surprise. The U.S. Navy had already signaled its intention to use southern Calvert County for amphibious landing training when a flotilla of ten to twenty landing barges showed up off Solomons in early spring, 1942. For a dozen property owners in the tiny watermen's community, the Navy's arrival brought eviction notices giving the owners an uncompromising twenty-four hours to vacate and move all their possessions out of their homes and barns on the peninsula at the end of Dowell Road. The dispossessed included prominent businessman and yacht club co-founder Halvor Hellen, as well as the estate of John F. Webster, Cook Webster's deceased older brother. They won a thirty-day extension after a court appeal.

Rekars Hotel, next door to the Websters' store on Solomons Island, was one of the properties leased by the Navy until barracks were built on about 110 acres between Back Creek and Mill Creek, near the mouth of the Patuxent.

Farther north on the Bay, the invasion of Cove Point Beach was quite different. The Army rented one of the first summer cottages built on the beach, between Chesapeake and Webster Drives, to use as officers' quarters. On the south side of the house, the military erected a tall, wooden observation tower, from which all the ships, landing craft, and assault boats could be observed, as well as all activities on the beach.

THE MARTIN FAMILY

Sisters Kathy and Mary Ellen Martin were in their pre-teens in 1942 when the Martin family moved first to Baltimore and then to Cove Point from Duluth, Minnesota, with their six children, each less than two years apart. Mary Ellen, second youngest, recalls Maryland was "not as cold" as Minnesota, where she'd never seen any Black people. So when they arrived in Baltimore, where the Great Migration accounted for a multiracial population, and she saw a Black person for the first time, she'd asked her dad if all the people there would have tinted skin. He said no.

Her father, Chad Walter Martin, was one of a half-dozen electricians transferred from the aircraft manufacturing giant Glenn L. Martin Company's Baltimore plant to southern Maryland at the start of World War II. Their job was to build airplane hangars at the Patuxent Naval Air Station, in neighboring St. Mary's County. Chad and his wife, Emily, rented a house at Cove Point Beach, one of a handful of cottages built shortly after the opening of the new community, just two short, wooded blocks from the beach. John Lusby, a local builder, had bought four adjacent lots on Park Drive, near the corner of Lighthouse Boulevard, and built his two-story, white cottage with a screened porch on two of them. Not least of all, the cottage had electricity and an indoor toilet, two things, Mary Ellen recalls, many of the houses in Solomons lacked.

To the kids, it was one big playground. Both Kathy and Mary Ellen recall walking the beach during the summer before the soldiers arrived, and hunting for fossils, especially shark teeth. Finding these ancient relics was "so commonplace," Kathy recalls, that when as an adult she was cleaning out her house in preparation for a move, she'd tossed out a whole boxful.

They also learned to swim in the cove's safe waters. Kathy says, "We knew not to swim at the Point where there was a dangerous rip current." And they played on the fishing pier, where their oldest sibling, brother Bill (born in 1923), taught them to dive.

Martin siblings, Betty, Mary Ellen, Bill, Kathy, Irene, and Dorothy at Cove Point during World War II. (Courtesy Martin family)

Bill had tried to enlist three times but was rejected due to a kidney condition that used to be known as Bright's disease. Finally, the Navy accepted him, and he was assigned to the SS *Fitzhugh Lee*, a Liberty ship built to carry cargo and military supplies.

More than a year after the Japanese bombed Pearl Harbor and the U.S. entered the war, life at Cove Point Beach changed dramatically. "Once the soldiers arrived," Kathy recalls, "we were no longer allowed to go near the water." But unlike those Solomons owners who were forced to evacuate, Cove Point Beach residents (few in number at the time) were allowed to stay. Mary Ellen recalls that a Navy family—the McStays—rented the house on the beach at the end of Park Drive, where she babysat their two little girls. She also recalls the guardhouse the Army set up on Cove Point Road, at the top of the hill, opposite the Hagelins' house, to turn away nonresidents.

A BOY AND HIS BIKE

Bob Wilson, just nine years old at the start of World War II, recalls having no problem rolling past the checkpoint on his bicycle, after speeding past the tomato cannery, then flying like a raptor down the hill to meet up with his friends. His buddies at that time were Wallace and Jackie, the sons of first assistant lighthouse keeper Zadock Sturgis. An ancestor, William James Wilson, had come to Calvert County from Scotland in 1674. (Most of those early records were lost, he notes, when the courthouse in Prince Frederick burned down in 1882, but some local churches had records of their own.) His father,

William James Wilson, owned a farm about a mile north of St. Paul's Methodist Church, on what is now Trueman Road (where the elementary school is today) in what was then known as Bertha. Wilson and his brother (Uncle Alvin) sold 140 acres that had been in the family for decades to the Boy Scouts in 1931 for $3,000. It became Camp Canoy.

Uncle Alvin was the first member of the family to go to college (one of the reasons they used to call him "rich Uncle Alvin"). Another uncle, Rayner Wilson, was a blacksmith, whose shop was near the current elementary school, on the opposite side of the road. Today, some of the old Wilson farm where Bob grew up belongs to Exelon Corporation, owner of Calvert Cliffs Nuclear Power Plant. Somebody, he says, desecrated the old family graveyard, knocking over or destroying tombstones. "We don't know who."

Bobby Wilson's playground was Cove Point. Bobby and the lighthouse kids all went to public school in Solomons (in what is now the Calvert Marine Museum), and became buddies in Sunday school at St. Paul's. Sunday school, he recalls, "was where my social life began."

More than seven decades later, Bob Wilson's recollections of those days before the invasion are not much different from the Martin sisters' memories. The boys also liked to run up the lighthouse steps all the way to the lamp, until assistant lighthouse keeper Sturgis put a stop to it. Once the war began, Sturgis "always had the radio on to get war news" and didn't pay much attention to the kids, "unless we did something wrong that got us into trouble."

One of the boys' favorite adventures was exploring the ponds and marshes north of the lighthouse, especially when they caught a large turtle. They were also aware of the danger of entering the water on the south side of the lighthouse, even to wade. He recalls an incident in the late 1940s when lighthouse keeper James Somers rowed out into the Bay to assist in a futile attempt to rescue a woman and her young child who'd been dragged out by the rip current. Other than that, Bob Wilson can recall nothing bad happening at Cove Point in those halcyon summer days.

Once the soldiers arrived, the kids' daily romps on the beach came to an end. "As kids, nobody bothered us," Wilson recalls, "but when they were practicing landings, we were kept off the beach. The military acted like the 'mayor' during that training." He also remembers the army asking locals to open their homes to the workers who came to the county to build the base in Solomons:

> *Many were men from Virginia and West Virginia who hadn't had decent jobs in years due to the Depression. Some people would rent out a bedroom where a couple of men would stay.*

One man, Wilson recalls, lived in an abandoned bus. A group of Navy wives set up a register of affordable housing in the county "to give couples a chance to be together before the husband goes overseas," and in certain more populated areas, "to aid housewives by eliminating the innumerable doorbell and telephone room hunters."

"WAR" IN THE FRONT YARD

Army troops, vehicles, and equipment on Cove Point Beach in front of bungalows. (Courtesy U.S. National Archives)

Kathy Martin vividly recalls the soldiers rolling onto the sand in trucks after spilling out of the bows of huge amphibious landing ships, known as "ducks," for training maneuvers. Soon there were foxholes all around their house, "but we weren't allowed to go near them."

Kathy's mother, looking out the window, sadly noted how young many of the soldiers were—some even younger than her own son, Bill. She decided to make soup and sandwiches for as many as she could. She wanted to treat these young men just as she would like someone to treat her first-born, who was by then a gunner on the SS *Fitzhugh Lee*, somewhere out at sea. A visit from a commanding officer put an end to it. He told her she had to stop.

"But they're just kids," she pleaded.

"They're going to war"—where no one will be cooking like that for them, he answered. "They have to get used to K-rations."

Some of the soldiers had their own ideas about that, and would trade K-rations for a sandwich or snacks from the Martin kitchen. Kathy recalls the girls thought the rations were delicious and happily made the trades. The girls would also run up to a small shack at the south end of the cove where, before the invasion, George Hagelin had collected parking fees for what was then a public beach, and now kept candy and other snacks for sale over the counter. The soldiers weren't allowed to go there themselves, but the kids were happy to make these runs. Mary Ellen also recalls soldiers sneaking her, Kathy, and their sister Dorothy into the commissary at Dowell Road, which was off-limits.

The soldiers encamped around their house also enjoyed reading the family's home-delivered *Washington Post,* so much so that Mary Ellen recalls "when Daddy came home from work in the evening, he had to go about retrieving the various sections that had been passed around by the soldiers."

And sometimes, the soldiers would get a little fresh. She specifically remembers one calling out that she must have a great singing voice—"because you've got legs like a canary!"

The older girls, who were in their mid-teens at the time, had different reactions to the soldiers' proximity to their house than their younger sisters. When their mom did the family wash, it was the girls' responsibility to hang it out on the clothesline to dry. Since the wet laundry included their bras and panties, the girls were embarrassed to do this chore with the soldiers around, so they paid their younger siblings to do it. Kathy recalls with a laugh, "I was happy to take their coins!"

One day, sister Betty was driving the family's '39 Plymouth out of the driveway when one of the huge "ducks" backed into them. Kathy believes her sister was chauffeuring her and Irene to Our Lady Star of the Sea in Solomons, as she did before the school acquired a bus. (Before Betty got her license, the girls were picked up by pastor Father Alexander's housekeeper, Miss Helen Chambers.) Mary Ellen's recollection is that her mother was in the car and they were headed to the grocery store. Either way, the sisters agree that the military driver apologized, saying he hadn't seen them, and that the army would pay for the damage to the car's grille. Neither recalls that happening.

The Martin sisters remember the evenings when there was a knock at the door. "The commanding officer would be standing there," Mary Ellen recounts, "and he would say, 'we're having a battle tonight.'" He would instruct them to stay inside and keep their windows and doors shut tight to keep out the tear gas that would be released.

"But since the windows weren't very tight, some of the gas would seep in and have all of us in tears." They were also required to have blackout shades in the windows.

Says Mary Ellen, "It felt like war."

Two soldiers in a foxhole at Cove Point Beach. (Courtesy U.S. National Archives)

They were called "routine" training maneuvers, but the fact that they were still rife with danger became apparent to everyone on Saturday, August 12, 1944, when a plane from the Patuxent River Naval Air Station, conducting a simulated air strike, crashed into the bow of a Navy ship off Cove Point. The ship was carrying plebes from the Naval Academy, two of whom were killed, along with the pilot and a WAVE (a member of the women's branch of the U.S. Naval Reserve) in the aircraft. The maneuver was part of a program in which planes came in at low altitude and fired blank bullets at the amphibious-type craft in order to give the midshipmen training in repelling such attacks. The Navy said it was not known whether the crash was a result of pilot error or an air current in which the plane may have been caught.

Explosion behind soldier on Cove Point Beach. (Courtesy U.S. National Archives)

BEYOND THE COVE

Throughout the war and post-war period, a new weekly newspaper, the *Calvert Independent*, launched in October 1940, kept residents informed about local developments such as the county Department of Education's sponsorship of canning centers in 1944. A year later, the paper urged "canning of every garden tomato that does not go on the family table." As the U.S. entered what would be the last year of the war, a War Food Administration leaflet urged "Keep canning!" Shorter supplies of some foods had resulted in stricter rationing on everything from meats to cooking oils, and canned fruits and tomatoes. In addition to home-canning, the newsletter urged use of the community canning centers that had been set up in many towns, including Lusby, on Cove Point Road, where families could use large pressure canners for processing home-produced food or vegetables and fruits for canning, with help from a trained person on preparing and packing the food for processing.

Calvert Independent articles urged farmers to sign up for a planned Freezer Locker Plant in Prince Frederick, which reportedly could save them twenty-five to fifty percent of food costs. A series of articles followed the test run of the plant, in October 1947, as well as a full-page ad offering to "kill, chill, age, cut, wrap and quick freeze at 20 degrees below Zero." The articles included instructions on how to prepare meats for freezing, advising to "bleed birds" and be sure to label packages, noting that freezing was new to many as a food preservation method. A large, front-page article in December announced that the Freezer Locker Plant was now offering butchering service, having already butchered and frozen almost 300 hogs. The plant specified, however, that "no hogs over 400 lbs." would be handled.

All of this, the canneries, the Freezer Locker Plant, and other such measures were used to counter a hard year for Calvert farmers in 1946. The *Independent* reported that the large crop sold in 1945 was sandwiched between a very poor crop sold in 1944 and a "crop disaster" coming in 1946.

The paper also ran front page ads urging limited use of long-distance telephone service so as to keep available lines accessible, and "rounding up" of scrap metal. The ads noted that fifty percent of all new steel needed for weapons and other war materiel was made from scrap.

Calvert Independent ad calls for scrap iron.

Pens and pencils were among the many products covered by price control, which made it illegal to sell them and other goods without a proper tag imprinted with the ceiling price. Clothing, notably rayon stockings, headed the list of shortages, a government newsletter observed, concluding on the cheery note that summer was coming, and "we can always join the bare-legged crowd." Shortages of copper and copper-based alloys affected the availability of zippers and snap fasteners for clothing. The result, at least in women's clothing, was more wrap-around styles fastened with bows or buttons.

The *Calvert Independent* supported a contest sponsored by the Office of Price Administration in which students wrote essays on "How Price Control Has Helped My Family." The paper reported the first ($100), second ($50) and third ($25) prize winners in the county's "White" (Calvert) and "Colored" (Brooks) high schools.

By 1945, there were shortages in all areas, including cars for civilians, tires and fuel. The Office of Defense Transportation even asked that schools at all levels cancel spring vacations to make space on trains and buses, normally used by some 300,000 students, available for more urgent transportation.

BACK TO NORMAL

There was a period without the military presence at both the beginning and the end of the Martin family's stay at Cove Point Beach.

After the soldiers left, the family roasted oysters in the foxholes they left behind. Kathy joined Virginia Sadler, her same age and the daughter of the next assistant lighthouse keeper, Charles Sadler, for good times playing at the lighthouse. And, like little Bobby Wilson, they were stopped in their tracks before they could run to the top.

When housing became available in Solomons, Chad Martin decided it was time to move his family closer to his job at Pax River. From Solomons, he and other workers were ferried across by Leon Langley and other watermen, as well as the Navy, since there was at the time no bridge across the river from Calvert County.

By 1946, Bob Wilson recalls that everything quieted down, and Solomons went back to being "a fishing place, with Bowen's the only inn." With the troops gone from Cove Point, he went back to playing on the beach with his buddies. One day they found a large can of K-rations in the sand and hung it over a fire. It exploded, sending beans flying everywhere. "We thought someone was trying to kill us!"

In 1960, beachcombers found four live, barnacle encrusted rockets, each about thirty inches long and four and a half inches in diameter, washed up on the beach north of the lighthouse. An Army information officer described the rockets as a "barrage" type used during the war to shell beaches before troops landed. Demolition experts from Fort Meade picked them up and gingerly placed them in field ammunition bunkers, to be blown up later. The LaPadula kids found ordnance behind their grandparents' house on Lighthouse Boulevard (next door to where the Martins had lived) in the late 1960s; their parents were happy it wasn't live.

7

THE FIFTIES

Life was good!

The *Calvert Independent* couldn't have been more explicit in its opposition to a Maryland state legislator's 1945 proposal for a state park in southern Calvert at either Drum Point or Lusby, north of St. Leonard Creek. A front-page editorial argued that anyone who wanted to enjoy the Bay should buy a lot or two down here.

"According to tradition, Calvert County is part of the Garden of Eden," the writer asserted, telling of a man who had a dream that he'd died and gone to heaven where, when it was his turn to be registered, St. Peter asked him where he had lived.

"When he answered that he was from Calvert County, St. Peter looked him right in the eye and said, 'My child, go back to Calvert County, for you never will be satisfied in heaven.'"

THE RYANS AND MILLERS

Whether they read that editorial or not, Washingtonians toward war's end were looking to Calvert once again for a pleasant place to escape the humid summer heat, cast a line in the water, and let their children run free on a beach. Chuck Miller recalls his family driving down to Cove Point from Northeast D.C. in the 1950s to visit his grandparents, the Ryans, at their beach house, with its covered porch on two sides, nestled on the corner of Beach Drive and Lighthouse Boulevard. His parents and his dad's mother, Agnes Miller, had also bought lots on Lighthouse Boulevard in the mid-1940s, after being advised by Grandpa Ryan that lots on the beachfront were not as desirable because of "all the sand blowing into the house."

Back in D.C., Grandpa and Uncle Bill Ryan were making history as the capital's last craft bookbinders, described by the *Evening Star* as "vestiges of a highly specialized profession dating back to Roman times." It was an intricate craft, in which each section of pages was separately stitched before all were sewn together, resulting in not only a custom product, often covered in an exquisite leather, but one that would outlast manufactured counterparts three-to-one. And all this at a comparable price.

The Ryans' clients included the federal courts, museums, government agencies, academia, law libraries, embassies and private citizens. Grandson Chuck Miller proudly recalls binding his girlfriend's missal while working there one summer. The shop was in the shadows of Catholic University, near the site of the future viaduct, and the Heckman's Pickle factory (the only one in D.C.) at 811 Monroe Street NE, next to the railroad tracks. His grandmother, Mary D. Ryan, worked at the nearby Franciscan Monastery.

But the bookbinding business was fast becoming almost totally automated. When both Ryans were ready to retire, their next generation was not interested in carrying on the fifty-year-old business. So when they closed the shop, the Ryans donated its historic equipment to the Smithsonian.

It was neither bookbinding nor any other business that had drawn the Ryans to the new community at Cove Point Beach in their younger days. Living above their shop at 709 Michigan Avenue NE, father and son shared the desire to find a comfortable place for wife and mother during the hot summer months. Grandpa was also an avid fisherman who had explored a number of places on the Chesapeake Bay, including Cove Point, where he'd found the best surfcasting beach of any of the places he'd been. In February 1945, he and his son bought three adjacent lots and promptly built a cottage on a corner with the main road.

Chuck Miller recalls the kids' anticipation as his father, Charles T. Miller, Sr., drove the family to Cove Point. He and his sisters, Kathleen and Eileen, had a contest to see who was first to spot St. Paul's Church at the intersection of Old Solomons Island and Cove Point Roads, and then who would see the Bay first from the top of the hill. In those days, that was easy, as the trees were not as tall as today. He recalls the privately owned "public" beach off to the right as they reached the bottom of the hill. George Hagelin, who delivered the daily newspaper, would usually be out there to collect a parking fee for beach use.

Grandmother Ryan depended on her son to bring them anything they needed, as she didn't have a car at the beach. Since both senior Ryans worked at the family business, Chuck's uncle could take off midweek, bring down some supplies, and do a little fishing before returning to D.C. Then he'd come back for the weekend, when Chuck and his sisters rode along on the weekly trip to the Solomons ice house for large blocks to refill the icebox. Chuck's parents and his uncle and grandparents were friends with the Dalys, who had purchased one of the first lots in the community, in June 1936. Their cottage at Beach Drive is visible in the World War II amphibious landing photos. John Daly had worked in the War Department (later renamed Department of Defense) before joining the General Accounting Office.

Chuck's best memories are of the good times when the extended Irish family, including all the young cousins, gathered for picnics on the beach, cheering on Uncle Bill as he swam out to a duck blind about a hundred feet from shore, and then climbed on top for a victory wave.

THE LaPADULAS

Already enjoying the cove even before the Ryans and Millers arrived, the LaPadulas bought their first property on Lighthouse Boulevard in 1941. Michael, an investigative accountant for the Securities and Exchange Commission, and his wife, Connie, had driven down the Chesapeake shore for picnics at various beaches every Sunday, looking for just the right spot until they came upon Cove Point. One glimpse of the pristine, white sand beach, stretching from north to south with outstretched arms forming a tranquil hollow, a natural harbor, left them no doubt.

Son Paschal (known as Pat) and his wife Mary followed five years later, buying the lot on the corner of Park and Lighthouse, and building the home their children and grandchildren enjoy today.

On left, Pat and Mary LaPadula. On right, "Party Animals" Michael and Connie LaPadula at Cove Point. (Courtesy Karin LaPadula)

More than seven decades later, third generation Karin LaPadula, an artist in Seattle, recalls growing up at Cove Point as if it were yesterday. Her grandparents, she says, were "party animals," part of a group of about six retired couples that had cocktail parties every Friday, and took turns hosting.

We used to spy on them when it was my grandparents' turn to host the group on their porch. One of the couples was known as 'The Girls,' which I only later realized was a lesbian couple. They were totally integrated and accepted into the group. Because the group didn't think anything of it, neither did we. Cove Point has always been gay friendly.

As children and teenagers, we used to explore the abandoned blue cottages (the Cove Point Club properties) where Cove of Calvert is now. One cottage had a white horizontal line painted about one foot up from the concrete floor in the dining room, with the writing: 'High- water mark, 1933.' My boyfriend took a photo of me standing in the doorway of that cottage. We used to skip school at University of Maryland, and drive to Cove Point for the day, even in the winter. That's when the photo was taken.

Karin LaPadula in doorway of abandoned Cove Point Club cottage. (Courtesy Karin LaPadula)

My brother and I used to hang out with the Harry brothers, Dave, Doug and Donnie. [Their father, Don Harry, was another early settler in Cove Point in 1940.] There were also some local guys who used to run with us. We'd drink beer on the beach, and sometimes even skinny dip. Every weekend, we went to the teen dance at the Chesapeake Ranch Club. Matt Calvin and I often won the dance contest and $15 each. I have great memories of my teenage summers at Cove Point, and the fun and freedom we had.

Karin is certain that the most magical night scene at Cove Point is from directly beneath the lighthouse, while sitting on the seawall, with the spokes of light rotating overhead. "My sister Susan and her friend showed this to me one night."

I sat there once when it was raining, and it looked like each spoke of light was full of glittering stars.

"Hole in the Sky" by Karin LaPadula, a memory of magical nights at Cove Point. (Courtesy Karin LaPadula)

Susan, now an Annapolis attorney, echoes the sentiment, adding, "It is magical, and full moons over the water at Cove Point have always been the best."

THE TUVE FAMILY

Maxine Duvel's father, a botanist and senior official at the U.S. Department of Agriculture, was more than pleased with the boyfriend she'd invited to spend a summer weekend with the family at Cove Point in 1934. The Duvels were renting one of the Cove Point Club's cottages on the beach at the south end of the hollow. A tall, handsome, young man, Richard Tuve was obviously in love with Duvel's daughter, and quickly became smitten as well with everything the Cove had to offer—the swimming, fishing, and most of all, the serenity along the miles of shoreline. The couple married two years later, after which Richard embarked on a stellar career with the Naval Research Laboratory. Among his credits, development of a chemical sea dye surface marker for survivors of air and ship disasters in World War II.

The Tuves bought a lot in a newly opened, third section of Cove Point Beach in 1951. They were disappointed at first when the Glascocks' real estate agent told them there were no lots for sale on the beach, and instead offered them one in the second tier. The agent's instructions were to sell the properties at a ratio of three off-beach for every beachfront lot. But when Tuve showed him the meticulous building plans for their vacation home, the agent suddenly made a waterfront lot available.

Tuve cottage on the beach. (Courtesy Christine Tuve Burris)

Their house on the beach was ready for move-in by the following summer, just in time for the first Cove Point Citizens Association picnic in 1952.

Residents watch four-year-old Christine Tuve (below, far right) and other children preparing for the sack race, officiated by Michael LaPadula. (Courtesy Christine Tuve Burris)

Richard Tuve sometimes took the kids down to the clay cliffs at the west end of the cove in his aluminum motorboat, bypassing the fallen trees that made the area difficult to reach on foot. After enjoying the view from a high perch, Cove Point kids for decades would return home covered head-to-toe in the grey clay, hoping for a look of horror from mom before hosing it off.

Christine and Rik Tuve on the cliff. (Courtesy Christine Tuve Burris)

The danger of playing on or beneath the cliffs did not become apparent until decades later when a sudden landslide took the life of a twelve-year-old girl as she walked a few yards behind her parents on the Chesapeake Ranch Club beach in 1996.

While brother Rik mastered the art of sailing, Christine enjoyed riding her bicycle from one end of the community to the other, stopping for breaks at Ken and Jean Cornwell's, who happened to have the only television in the cove in the early '50s. "These were," she sighs, "unforgettable times."

THE BRANNANS

As a division chief in the U.S. Treasury Department, accountant Charles Brannan knew how to handle money. His proudest achievement was teaching his seven children not only how to manage theirs but also how to earn it from an early age—nine years old, to be exact. That's when each of his four oldest sons started delivering the *Washington Star* in their suburban neighborhood of Mount Rainier, Maryland. His two daughters would soon follow in their brothers' footsteps, as would their youngest brother who, at two years old, could already pull a newsboy's wagon. Seventy years later, Francis "Frannie" Brannan recalls that he did so well signing up new customers in the late 1940s, he earned the reward of a day at his boss's Cove Point Beach summer cottage.

When Frannie returned home, his description of the beach was so enthusiastic his parents drove down to see it for themselves. That was all they needed. Charles and Anna bought the real estate agent's office on Holly Drive in 1953, and added to it over the next half-century.

The family's ninety-minute drive from Mount Rainier on Friday evenings in the family's 1937 Chevy zipped by quickly until they reached St. Leonard, about ten miles from their destination. Then it was Daddy's turn to relax, have "a nip" at a cozy little bar (still there), and play the slots for a few minutes while the kids rooted for him to win. (Calvert was one of four southern Maryland counties that licensed the machines. Some localities became so heavily dependent on them that by 1963, state legislators, worried that gambling was taking over the southern Maryland economy, gave the counties five years to phase them out.)

As her brood grew up, Anna Brannan returned to work, first as a justice of the peace in nearby Prince George's County, and then as census supervisor for six Maryland counties, including Calvert. Responsible for hiring the door-to-door census takers for the upcoming population count, the mother of seven successful news boys and girls told reporters she was looking for applicants with "salesmanship," a talent she and her husband had obviously cultivated in their own children. Over the next decade, the Brannans would play active roles in the growing beach community.

Looking back over those early years, from the pit stop in St. Leonard to their beach bungalow at Cove Point and the weekend runs down to Solomons pier for movies and ice cream, Frannie Brannan says southern Maryland seemed like the end of the world to the Brannan kids. "Life was good."

CHANGE A-COMIN'

While the LaPadulas, Brannans, Ryans, Millers, Dalys, Tuves, Wolkonskys, and a dozen or so other "first" families enjoyed the peace of the cove on summer days in the mid-1950s, a very different scene was playing out about 1,000 feet north of the lighthouse, on a part of the shoreline that Cove Pointers called "the north beach." In the early 1950s, beachcombers from the cove could walk around the lighthouse and continue north—not seeing another human being for miles—past the marshes to an isolated shoreline called Rocky Point. There, the meandering would finally be blocked by the trunks and branches of fallen trees where the cliffs rose up again and erosion took its toll. But by the end of the decade, without any warning, all of this serene solitude in the midst of the most incredible natural beauty, devoid of anything but God's own creations, came to a halt—an ultimately crashing halt.

8

THE BOTTOMLESS PIT

A scheme murkier than a muskrat marsh

Cook Webster's daughter must have pinched herself when she saw the offer. Sarah Catherine Glascock had inherited thousands of acres of prime farmland and forest from her late father in 1938. But the subject of this offer was a swamp. True, the parcel had a more euphemistic name—the Cove Point Cattail Marsh—but to locals it seemed a mosquito-infested swamp. And now, in 1952, a stranger from Silver Spring, Maryland, was proposing to lease it for the purpose of "excavating sands for the recovery of possible minerals found therein."

The offer came from a silver-haired civil engineer named Charles Jefferson who explained that he'd chosen the shoreline north of Cove Point after prospecting up and down the Atlantic Coast. His theory was that when sifted, the black particles of ilmenite and rutile in the sands of the beach north of the lighthouse would yield an abundance of titanium and zircon ores. Titanium was considered the new "wonder metal," rustproof, lighter than steel, stronger than aluminum, and in immediate demand in the aircraft industry. Zircon was valued for its use in ceramics and various manufacturing processes.

While titanium was the primary objective, another product would be calcium carbonate, produced by pulverizing the oyster, clam and other shells dredged up in the mining process.

CATTAIL MARSH

Besides a monthly rental fee, the Glascocks (Sarah and her husband William Bedford) included three conditions in the lease: Jefferson was to put back the non-mineral sands dug up along the shoreline as excavation progressed; his use and occupancy of an additional parcel of land (about 400 feet) adjoining the pond on the leased property must not interfere with the Glascocks' development of Cove Point Beach (the final section of which would not be platted until 1956); and the couple reserved the right "to trap for muskrat" in the leased marsh.

The muskrat season, running through the winter, was no joke along the marshes of the Chesapeake Bay. For decades, the skins of this large rodent, particularly the black ones, were valued for their soft, glossy fur, while their meat was also sold at market for human consumption. Appearing on menus in even the best restaurants, it was sometimes more appealingly offered as "marsh rabbit." Another legitimate label would be its original name, "musquash." Some compared its flavor to wild duck. Whatever it was called, it was very popular and the trapping very profitable, bringing sums as high as $2.5 million to Chesapeake counties in some years.

Jefferson was obviously pleased with what he found along the Cove Point shoreline in the months following execution of that initial lease in October 1952. The following year, he discussed with the Glascocks plans to form a corporation for further exploration and extraction of minerals at the site, as well as to construct a harbor or port on the premises. Jefferson saw an opportunity, while mining for the titanium, to make some immediate cash by selling the pulverized shells dredged up in the process to Bay area farmers right from the site. This idea may have come from the man he was partnering with in the mining operation, John Rogers, whose company, Tidewater Pier and Dredging in neighboring Anne Arundel County, would fabricate the heavy dredging and processing equipment.

THE PARTNER

Rogers had been something of a local celebrity in the waterside communities along the Bay since 1931, when *The Sun* ran a two-column article on the twenty-eight-foot, oak and cedar fishing boat the hobbyist was building under a tent in his Baltimore backyard. A year later, a follow-up article included a photo of Rogers with his completed cabin cruiser, ready for launch, although still in the backyard, six miles from the water. As it turned out, he was also launching a new career as a very successful boat builder.

In 1943, after a decade of producing pleasure craft, fishing boats and sleek racing yachts, Rogers was garnering more headlines for his wartime production of ship parts. An article in the *Evening Star* announced that Rogers was turning out parts for the Navy and merchant ships faster than any other shipyard in the country. The reason was his invention of a 100-foot spar lathe that produced in one hour as many spars as other yards with twice the number of employees were turning out in two days by hand.

Jefferson, on the other hand, was relatively unknown to Marylanders. He'd spent almost twenty years as a sand and gravel contractor in Indiana, where the only headlines he'd earned involved a couple of fruitless oil drilling operations and an indictment for conspiracy to defraud the U.S. government by diverting public labor and funds to private use. Unlike five associates who went to prison, he was acquitted on the grounds that he had lacked control over the money. The notoriety apparently was bad enough for him to leave Indiana, and resettle in Silver Spring, Maryland, after the case closed in 1941.

THE LAUNCH

Jefferson registered the Titanium Ores Corp. in the state of Maryland, with himself as president and John Rogers as vice-president, and assigned to it the Cattail Marsh lease. The new company's first stock issue immediately attracted press attention. The Associated Press reported that the Chesapeake Bay shore north of Cove Point was about to be prospected for titanium, "a highly sought and scarce metal." The article clearly stated that the prospectus accompanying the stock offer emphasized the "speculative" nature of the venture, adding that "No claim is made that the existence of a commercial deposit has been established."

Ads for the stock also plainly stated in bold print: "These shares are offered as a speculation."

New Issue

300,000 SHARES

TITANIUM

ORES
CORPORATION
COMMON STOCK ·
Price $1.00 per share

These shares are offered as a speculation

BUSINESS: The mining, dredging and processing of Titanium Ores (Ilmenite and Rutile).

LOCATION: The corporation's mineral properties are located near Cove Point, Calvert County, Maryland, in the vicinity of Calvert Cliffs.

┌─────**M. J. SABBATH CO.**─────┐
1627 K St. N.W., Wash. 6, D. C.   RE. 7-4313
Please send me copy of the TITANIUM offering circular

Name (Print) _____

Address _____

_____ Phone _____
└──────────────────────────────────┘

Ad: Titanium Ores Corp. Stock Offer: *Evening Star,* May 6, 1954

Cove Point residents accustomed to walking the beach in search of fossils washed out of the cliffs farther north were aware of the spotty black patches in the sands referenced in the Titanium Ores Corp.

prospectus, but had never given them much thought. Jefferson, however, was touting the find as if it were black gold. Several Cove Point property owners thought the venture might be worthwhile, as did prominent people all over the state.

Titanium Ores Corp. Stock Certificate

Stock sales continued through 1954, and may have received a boost from a *Washington Post* article in January 1955 which was much less cautious in its reporting about the venture than the AP article a year earlier. Under the headline "Titanium Found Along Chesapeake," the subhead reported in bold typeface: "Deposit May Yield 60 Tons Daily." The article led off with seven paragraphs detailing the value of, and demand for, the "wonder metal."

Describing Jefferson's plant as the first of its kind in the U.S. and the first commercial production of titanium ore in Maryland history, the article quoted the engineer as stating that when the mine began round-the-clock operations that spring, "about three tons of titanium ore will be produced every hour." Once any possible "operational bugs" were worked out, the article continued, the plant was "expected to produce 87,380 tons of ore annually." Nowhere did it suggest who, besides Jefferson, shared these expectations. The article included a photo of pipes and barrels stretching into the marsh, over a caption describing it as part of $300,000 worth of equipment that would be used in dredging and processing titanium, and repeating—without attribution—the expectation that "some 60 tons" would be produced daily by spring.

Rogers told the press in April 1955 that the special beach sand mining machinery would be going into operation at Cove Point in about four weeks. That fall and the following winter, ads were placed in local papers for immediate sales help for a new issue of common stock, saying the corporation was "swamped with leads," an interesting choice of words considering the mine's location in the marsh. A court document a few years later would reveal that the corporation netted over $200,000 from that stock sale, adding to assets of $107, 014 in machinery and equipment listed in the offering circular.

In March of 1957, with the operation apparently going well, Jefferson signed a new five-year lease with the Glascocks at higher rent. Two months later, Titanium Ores Corp. announced a public offering of

$250,000 in debentures, unsecured loan certificates. Again, despite the speculative nature of the project, the offering netted approximately $200,000.

Titanium Ores Corp. dredging operation north of Cove Point Lighthouse circa 1958. (Courtesy Calvert Marine Museum)

"IF NOT MORIBUND"

There were no visible signs of anything gone awry until 1958, when a major, but to this day mysterious, blow-up between Jefferson and Rogers revealed that operations in Cattail Marsh were mired in muck. While neither the courts nor the newspapers ever revealed the reason behind Jefferson's falling out with his vice president and major shareholder, Rogers had picked up his marbles and gone home. Among the things he took with him was the boat—named "T102"—that the corporation used for exploration of mineral deposits.

He had sold the twenty-six-foot hull to the corporation in 1954 for $1300, payable whenever, or not at all if the boat were later returned with Rogers' improvements intact. After the falling out, Rogers went to Solomon's Marina where the craft was berthed, and had it towed to his own boatyard. Titanium Ores sued to get it back. The trial court ruled in Rogers' favor, and Titanium Ores appealed. Upon review, the appellate court agreed with Jefferson, ruling that although at the time of the trial, Titanium Ores was in "low financial condition" and apparently could not pay Rogers the $1300 purchase price, the sale had been unconditional, with title passing to the corporation. The boat was returned to Titanium Ores.

The court laid the blame on Rogers, saying he had used Titanium Ores' ownership of the boat to attract investors, and could not deny that now, when the corporation was in "serious financial difficulty"—or even worse:

> *Individuals answered the inducements by investing and lending hundreds of thousands of dollars to a corporation which now appears to be struggling to continue, if not moribund. These owners in, and creditors of, the corporation have a right to have the boat be a part of the corporate assets, as it was represented to them to be.*

The Glascocks apparently were aware of the corporation's financial problems months before the court, in December 1959, described its financial condition as perhaps "moribund." They had signed a new agreement with Jefferson at a rental thousands of dollars lower than he had been paying. Later, there was another hint that things didn't look good when a news article about a controversial shell dredging contract proposed by the state of Maryland quoted one official as saying that Titanium Ores Corp. had been ruled out because it "would be unable to perform the work needed."

PROJECT BOOTSTRAP

An investor might never have gleaned any of this from the glowing statements put forth in the company's March 1961 "Annual and Progress Report to Stockholders." The report introduced a handful of prominent Maryland men as new officers and directors, while apparently taking a swipe at Rogers with the comment, "We are especially fortunate at last in having Directors and Officers who cheerfully accept the responsibilities delegated to them and aggressively pursue their fulfillment."

It also announced that the Board had authorized the sale of the remainder of common stock approved in December 1959. Included in the document was a metallurgical report that seemed to turn Jefferson's marketing spiel upside down. Calcium carbonate was no longer expected to be the byproduct from a rich titanium mine. It would be the principal product, and the ore, a maybe.

A retired Navy captain, newly appointed to the board, introduced the shareholders to "Project Bootstrap," leading off with the observation that most of the stockholders didn't understand the difficulties of this kind of mining operation. Suggesting that the new directors did, he revealed that several of them had pooled personal funds as an interest-free loan to the corporation to complete the plant. Reimbursement was to be in the form of common stock.

Under "Public Relations," the report invited all the shareholders "to enjoy the good beach and picnic facilities on the property of your corporation at Cove Point whenever you desire." It made no mention of the lack of any public facilities at the beach.

The final page was an appeal to something else in the human psyche. Under the headline "Foresight

Makes Millionaires!"—the board pointed to a vague history of mining investments as a source of great fortunes.

No mention of Titanium Ores Corp. or its mine at Cove Point appeared in the press again until November 1963, when Maryland's governor revoked the corporation's charter for failure to pay taxes.

The temptation here is to declare "end of story" and leave it to the reader as well as the investors who lost money to decide for themselves whether the operation was a serious miscalculation—based on equal parts incompetence and wishful thinking—or a greedy scam. But the story does not end here. The mystery deepens, until the pit appears bottomless.

"BY THE COMPANY HE KEEPS"

One suspicious oddity in Titanium Ores' 1961 annual report is a solicitation to its stockholders from a Maryland institution, the Military Service Savings and Loan Association, to open savings accounts. The letter from Military Service S&L ends with a declaration of "unqualified faith in the integrity and leadership" of Titanium Ores' officers and directors, the announcement of loans to the corporation, and commitments for more loans when and if needed. Immediately following that letter is a statement signed by Titanium Ores' new executive vice president, a retired rear admiral, stating that the corporation's three-member executive committee and its general counsel, having faith in the integrity of the S&L's officers, had each opened a savings account, and recommended the S&L as "a good, safe, lending institution."

Nine months later, November 1961, Military Service S&L was ordered into receivership by a Maryland court. Its president, Murray Michael, was charged with making loans to companies with which he was connected, issuing mortgages for more than the value of the property put up as security, and fraud. Titanium Ores' executive vice president acknowledged that he had served on the S&L's executive advisory board, having met Michael more than a year earlier while trying to raise financing for the mining operation. He said he was trying to save the S&L, as was Charles Jefferson, who admitted he'd negotiated a deal with Michael to obtain deposits for the S&L in exchange for mortgage loans to Titanium Ores.

Michael surprised the court in the middle of his trial by suddenly pleading guilty to fraud.

As of the time of his trial in April 1964, shareholders in his savings and loan had been repaid only twenty cents on every dollar invested. His original claim that its loans were fully protected by Security Financial Insurance Corp., a private firm, had been proven untrue in 1962, when the state placed the insurer in receivership. The grounds were insolvency and poor management. In his decision upholding the state's appointment of a receiver, the judge said he'd found ample evidence to support the contention that Security Financial was operating illegally and practicing fraud. Most of the firm's stock, he said, was originally issued to two Canadian companies that were "shrouded in mystery," its directors appearing to be mere figureheads carrying out the will of the unknown owners.

If you're wondering what Security Financial's demise in 1962 had to do with the titanium mine at Cove Point, read on.

In seeking to take over the insurer, the State had specifically charged that Security Financial's president, 33-year-old accountant K. George Christian, appointed in a management shake-up just six months earlier, was unqualified for the post, because of his lack of insurance experience. Now he was out of a job.

DIGGING DEEPER

Less than two years later, in April 1964, Christian (who had a law degree from the University of Maryland) was one of three incorporators of a Maryland company called "Space Minerals, Inc." Two weeks later, on May 1, 1964, the new company executed a 30-year lease with the Glascocks for the Cattail Marsh and surrounding acreage for mining operations. This was less than five months after Maryland's nullification of Titanium Ores' corporate charter. Whether any of the officers or directors of Titanium Ores had any involvement in the new Space Minerals operation is a mystery, but it seems likely since several had poured personal funds into the now defunct entity.

It also seems unlikely that any of the three incorporator/directors, including K. George Christian, was anything but a front for the real people behind the operation. It's difficult to "follow the money" when the trail begins and ends in a bottomless pit.

When Christian resigned as the company's resident agent just over a year later, no successor was appointed. There was no mention of Space Minerals or the Cove Point mine in the press until a notice, published in November 1966, that the Governor of Maryland had revoked its charter, too, for nonpayment of taxes. Charles Jefferson, coincidentally, had died earlier the same year.

On January 4, 1971, the Glascocks signed two sworn affidavits. One declared that no rents had been received from Jefferson since May 31,1963, and that his lease was therefore null and void; the other declared that the 1964 lease with Space Minerals had been terminated June 1, 1965. The affidavits preceded sale of the entire area covered by those terminated leases, plus about 1,000 additional acres, to Columbia Liquid Natural Gas (CLNG). It was the end of mining on Cove Point's north beach, and the beginning of a whole new era—with impact far beyond the tiny Cove Point Beach community.

9

THE EYE OF THE STORM

*The world beyond the cove
was a roiling sea.*

The 1960s changed America more than any other decade of the century. But if you lived in Cove Point Beach, you would only know what you saw in the news. Aside from the bizarre water rescue of a stowaway a few nautical miles north of the Cove Point Lighthouse, and the usual run of enthusiastic fishing reports, the metropolitan newspapers found nothing newsworthy in or around the Bayside colony during the entire decade. The water rescue that was the exception occurred on Labor Day, 1960.

In the hours before dawn, the Coast Guard received a weak radio message from the Venezuelan freighter *Ciudad de Cumana*, en route to Baltimore, that sounded as though the vessel had recovered a body from the warm, brackish waters just north of Cove Point. Actually, what the crew had spotted and rescued from the shipping channel was a live person. The man, in his mid-thirties, told the sympathetic seamen that he had survived the sinking of his fishing vessel. But investigators boarding the ship on its arrival in Baltimore already suspected the man's story would not hold water. When pulled from the

Bay, Nealson Fonseca had been clinging to a life preserver with markings from the Liberian motor ship *Delphic Eagle*. Unbeknown to his rescuers, that freighter had earlier reported to the Coast Guard that a Brazilian stowaway had jumped ship near Cove Point, between 1 and 5 a.m.

Facing a Baltimore jury in December, Fonseca changed his story entirely, testifying that he'd woken up on the *Delphic Eagle* not knowing how he'd gotten there. Since he'd been convicted of being a stowaway twice the previous year, he decided he shouldn't return to Baltimore. He swore that he'd slipped down a rope into the water in hopes of catching a ship going down the Bay and out to sea, away from another attempt to land illegally.

The jury didn't buy his story. The ship he'd waved down was also heading north to Baltimore. Convicted of illegally entering the country, Fonseca landed a one-year prison sentence.

A NEW BEGINNING

In Cove Point Beach, two events may not have been newsworthy, but they certainly were landmarks for the tiny community. One was the formation of a new property owners organization—the Cove Point Beach Association, Inc.—in 1961. The second, 16 months later, was Sarah and William Bedford Glascock's transfer of the roads in the community (with the exception of Lighthouse Boulevard, which they had conveyed to the county in 1947) to the new organization. They also granted the association the right to enforce covenants, collect the road maintenance fee, and enforce regulations regarding conduct of persons using the beach in the subdivision. (Actual ownership of the beachfront would be transferred in 1972.)

There already was an association of lot owners, called the Cove Point Citizens Association, founded in 1952. But as an unincorporated organization, it was not an appropriate entity to receive the roads deed from the heirs of founder J. Cook Webster. The new corporation was thus a legal necessity, and its articles of incorporation were signed by long-time community leaders Richard Tuve, Eugene Baczenas and Kenneth Cornwell.

As the last president of the Cove Point Citizens Association, Tuve invited members to its final meeting at Tuve Cottage on Sept. 3, 1962. He remained active in the colony's leadership for many years thereafter.

Baczenas and his wife, Marguerite, had bought one of the first lots in the development in 1938, on the beach at Chesapeake Drive. A prominent Catholic layman and management official with the Civil Service Commission, Baczenas was elected president of the new Cove Point Beach Association. In his first letter to its members, he confirmed that the Glascocks had conveyed to it ownership of the roads and the right to enforce the deeds to all properties in the colony.

Kenneth and Jean Cornwell had bought their first property in Cove Point Beach in 1953 but moved to what would become their full-time home on the beach, between Poplar and Hemlock, in 1956. Originally from Falls Church, Virginia, the affable community leader was famous for his fruit and vegetable gardens, from which he shared the largest, juiciest peaches, among other gems, ever coaxed from sandy soil. His other love was fishing, either from the shore in front of his ranch house, or his skiff, launched from the beach.

THE WORLD BEYOND THE COVE

Compared with the peace of the cove throughout the 1960s, the world beyond was a roiling sea of war, protest, confrontation, tragic loss, and historic victories. As the decade came to an end, everyone with a television witnessed Neil Armstrong's unforgettable "one small step" onto the surface of the moon, on July 20, 1969. It was also a decade of victory for seventeen African nations that gained their independence from colonial rule. But for the United States, it was a period of crises and tumult. In March 1960, the White House announced that 3,500 U.S. troops were being sent to Vietnam. As more and more deployments followed, countless protesters filled the streets in impassioned opposition to the war. Four students were shot dead and others wounded in what became known as the Kent State massacre, before the war finally came to an end in 1975, after the loss of more than 58,000 American soldiers. In 1962, the

Cold War between the U.S. and the Soviet Union sent school children ducking under their desks for shelter during the Cuban Missile Crisis, a thirteen-day political and military standoff over Soviet installation of nuclear missiles in Cuba. In 1963, a shocked and grieving nation mourned the loss of President John F. Kennedy, cut down by an assassin's bullet. Five years later, riots erupted across the country as outrage overcame mourning at the assassination of Dr. Martin Luther King, Jr. Two months later, the nation wept at the funeral of Senator Robert F. Kennedy, also the victim of an assassin's bullet.

It was the decade that ended eight frustrating years of a presidency that had urged Black Americans to be "patient" despite appallingly little progress toward racial justice. Calvert County's Black population had been paragons of patience. Former Calvert NAACP president Joyce Freeland recalls that everything in the county was still segregated in the early 1960s, even the county's only hospital, Calvert Memorial. As a child in the 1950s she'd been rushed there with a ruptured appendix. The hospital had no bed space for the four-year-old in the Black section, but because her condition was so serious (the doctor had given her a fifty percent chance of survival), she was treated in a laundry room.

A few Black students were permitted to attend Calvert High in the early 1960s, but they couldn't accompany their White classmates to other venues such as local restaurants after school. The Black high school, William Sampson Brooks, was closed in 1966, and all the Black students were enrolled in Calvert High. Calvert County NAACP president Michael Kent has traced his family history in the county back to 1779. He says that despite the 1954 Supreme Court decision declaring segregated schools unconstitutional, the county was still dragging its feet in the 1960s pending completion of a private school where many White families planned to send their children. That didn't happen until 1967.

As a result of the Jim Crow system, Blacks in Calvert County created an assortment of businesses of their own. It was no wonder then, as Christine Tuve Burris recalls, that her family was met with stares from other customers when her father pulled into a Black gas station on the drive to Cove Point in the late '50s. The family from D.C. was clearly not supposed to be there. When Richard Tuve invited Mr. Roberts, the Black handyman who helped him with projects around the house, to come in for a cold beer on a hot summer day, the older man politely demurred. He accepted the beer, but drank it on the front porch. That was custom. A Black man did not enter a White man's home, except as a servant.

The Tercentenary Edition of the *Calvert Independent* in 1954 had observed: "One of the most important situations in the County was the consideration and kindness with which they [Blacks] were treated throughout the pre- and post-slavery period." What the writer meant by the "pre-slavery" period is anybody's guess. He went on, however, to quote from nationally known author Hulbert Footner, who had done some of his writing in Solomons, in 1939:

> *There is an organized school system for his children. True, these schools are maintained out of negro taxes, which is unjust, since we keep him in a position where he can barely acquire any property to be taxed; still, he is subject to worse injustices elsewhere in our free country.*

It was the kind of thinking reflected in a history of Calvert County written by a retired school teacher in 2015, in which she mentioned "imported workers, or slaves as they were referred to."

Across the South, "patience" became an unacceptable blueprint. In Greensboro, North Carolina, four Black college students showed how little tolerance they had left for the local Woolworth store's refusal to serve African Americans at its "Whites-only" lunch counter. They sat down and refused to leave, touching off similar demonstrations across Dixie, where nonviolent activists endured pummeling, heckling, and even arrest to finally defeat Jim Crow, at least in that space. Another nonviolent civil rights protest on the campus of South Carolina State University in Orangeburg ended in a massacre, as state highway patrolmen fired into a group of 200 unarmed Black students, killing three and wounding twenty-eight.

In May 1961, Black and White civil rights activists, schooled in nonviolent protest, boarded two interstate buses in Washington, D.C. and sat in front seats. In the South, where they were headed, those seats by custom were reserved for White passengers, and the facilities in bus terminals where they would stop were segregated as well, despite U.S. Supreme Court decisions ruling such practices unconstitutional. The first of those buses, a Greyhound, was firebombed by a mob outside Anniston, Alabama. The second, a Trailways bus one hour behind, was boarded in the same town by White thugs who beat the Freedom Riders bloody and piled their bodies in the aisle. A Black reporter on that bus phoned Attorney General Robert Kennedy when they arrived in Birmingham to warn that the Freedom Riders were likely to be killed by the Klan unless he sent help to evacuate them. He did.

Twenty years later, that same Black reporter, Simeon Booker, who had covered every major event of the civil rights movement, ten U. S. presidents, and the Vietnam war, would also be the first Black man to purchase a property in Cove Point Beach.

Born in Baltimore in 1918, Booker, *Jet* and *Ebony* magazines' Washington Bureau Chief, had a favorite way to relax when he wasn't covering a story. It was fishing. And his favorite place to do it was on the Chesapeake Bay. A group of long time residents hosted a reception for Booker and his wife (this author). Their message was simple: Welcome to Cove Point!

10

THE DEVIL'S GRASP

It was like fingers pulling me down.

Joseph Cook Webster's quarter-page newspaper ads hawking Cove Point Beach lots proudly boasted that here was the "finest beach" on the great Chesapeake Bay. And it was true. The white sand, the gently sloping shoreline, the usually calm, clear waters—all contribute to a safe environment for a family swim within the embrace of a sandbar to the east and Little Cove Point to the southwest. Even when the cove is not calm, when waves roll in, crashing on the shore,

Aerial photo of Cove Point by Shawn Carroll, April 2020, shows the beach between the sandbar and the lighthouse where the rip current grasps its victims on incoming tides.

it is still not a dangerous beach. But that is within the cove. The devil, as became apparent over the years, has been next door.

Abutting Cove Point Beach to the northeast is the lighthouse property, including a small beach, usually delineated at the water line by the sandbar stretching out into the Bay. Sometimes the bar is visible for a hundred feet or more, and sometimes it's totally submerged but still outlined by wave action, depending on the season, the tide, the winds. The effect is a natural boundary between the two beaches.

THE FAMILY PICNIC, SEPTEMBER 14, 1947

There were brief articles in all the expected newspapers that week—*The Washington Post, Evening Star, New York Times* and, of course, the victims' hometown paper, the *Minneapolis Star-Tribune*. The first accounts reported the drownings of a mother and her four-year-old daughter in the waters near the Cove Point Lighthouse. Follow-up articles reported the ongoing search for the child's body. Other important details, such as how or why the tragedy happened, were never provided.

Jesse Anne ("J.A.") Foley, a graduate of Connecticut College, had married a Frenchman, Paul Blanc, in her hometown of St. Paul, Minnesota, in 1938. They had moved to France where both worked with the French underground during the war. During those years, J.A. gave birth to two children, Mary Ann (nicknamed "Bab"), in 1940, and Elizabeth ("Zizi"), in 1943. After the war's end in Europe in 1945, Paul was appointed financial counselor at the French embassy in Washington, D. C. In 1946, the couple celebrated the birth of a son, Frederick Foley Blanc, named after J.A.'s father.

Mother Drowns As Attempt to Save Child Fails

Embassy Official's Family Victims Of Beach Tragedy

The Evening Star, Sept. 15, 1947, p. 17.

Sunday, September 14, was a typically warm, humid day in Washington, but it was balmy and delightful on the Chesapeake Bay. Paul and J.A. loaded the kids in the car and drove down to Cove Point for a beach party with friends near the Cove Point Lighthouse. The property was owned by the federal government, while the lighthouse was manned by a civilian keeper, James Somers, who'd been in the post since 1943, and first assistant Charles Sadler, who'd joined him in 1944. Both had families living with them at the light. There were no fences around the lighthouse property. Facing east across the Bay, the site included a relatively secluded beachfront on its south side, running a hundred yards or so between the lighthouse and the long, narrow sandbar stretching out into the Bay.

Years later, in the 1980s, a weather-worn wooden sign warning "No Swimming" was visible well above the high-water line, but with no indication of when it was erected. Beyond the sandbar, the shore cut back to the southwest, forming a crescent shaped cove— Cove Point Beach.

One can imagine the Blancs and their friends on the beach, picnic baskets open on the blankets, the little ones being fed first, some of the adults scouring the shoreline for shells and fossils, others basking in the end-of-summer sun. The reports of the tragedy that came next reveal none of that. That's understandable. Just the facts. But the fact that was missing was why.

As reported in the newspapers, four-year-old Zizi "slipped off into deep water and her mother plunged in after her." Bob Wilson, fourteen years old at the time, who played with the Sadlers' children at the light, recalls that lighthouse keeper Somers joined in the rescue attempt, rowing a small skiff out into the Bay. But he was too late.

The indisputable fact missing from the accounts is that when little Zizi "slipped," she was actually being pulled by a rip current that swept her tiny body out from the shallows so fast that her mother, plunging in after her, was unable to reach the child, or possibly even see her, in the rolling surf of an incoming tide. J.A. herself, although just 35, would have been no match for the current. It took an hour for would-be rescuers to recover her body. J.A.'s funeral was delayed for days, awaiting the recovery of Zizi's body from rough Chesapeake waters.

A rip current has been called the ocean's "deadliest trick." This applies to the Chesapeake Bay, as well. The lighthouse beach is host to a treacherous one. Experts say it is easy to be caught in a rip current, and that it happens most often in waist-deep water, when the surf is pulling away from the beach. Breaking waves—not necessarily large—are the first, and to the untrained eye, sometimes the only clues. Without the waves, say the experts, there is no rip current.

Ranging from 50 to 100 feet wide, the current, like an underwater bullet train, can move at speeds of more than five miles per hour, pulling a swimmer outwards 100 yards or more from shore in seconds. Such currents are routine occurrences on some beaches, while others are almost never haunted by these devils beneath the surface.

It is most likely that four-year-old Zizi was not swimming but wading in the shallow water, when the retreating surf pulled the shifting sand out from under her tiny feet, causing her to lose her balance and fall into the rip current. There is also an underwater ledge not far from the shore, where the bottom drops off suddenly. She may have unintentionally stepped off that ledge. Her little body was finally recovered a week later, washed ashore at Point No Point, about twenty-five miles south of Cove Point. She was buried beside her mother in St. Paul.

It would be almost four decades before another incident—this time a near-drowning—was reported at the Point. It was not a public beach; swimming, whether or not a sign was posted, was not permitted. But it was accessible from Cove Point Beach, and the devil was waiting.

THE TWINS, AUGUST 24, 1983

It was a Wednesday, so there were fewer people on the beach than on a warm weekend in late summer. Blonde and tanned, Clarissa Sheridan was walking toward the Point from her house in Cove Point Beach with her two sons, Brian, almost four, and Jacob, six. The boys wanted to search for fossil shark teeth, and the sandbar jutting out into the Bay was the best hunting ground. It was about a ten-minute walk without interruptions, but the boys would prolong it with forays into the water, tag matches in the sand, and their "discoveries" (running up to mom with an oddly shaped stone or shell, inquiring, "is this a tooth?"). Sheridan didn't mind; it was a beautiful day and she was with her treasures.

As they approached the sandbar, she saw two little boys, just a few years older than her sons, step into the water on the north side. The surf was not rough, but there were waves. For some reason, she kept her eyes on those boys, and quickly realized they were too far from shore. She ran into the shallow water and called to them, "You're out too far—COME BACK!"

Their shrill response sent a chill down her spine. "We can't!"

Without a second thought, Sheridan jumped into the water. But as soon as she felt the current, she knew she could not swim in it. She had just stepped off the sandbar when suddenly, "It was like fingers pulling me down." She turned, lurching crosswise toward the bar until she felt the sand under her feet again, and stumbled to safety. Looking for help, she yelled to her older son to run to the lighthouse and get the Coast Guardsmen on duty there. (Coast Guardsmen had replaced the last civilian lighthouse keeper at Cove Point in 1958.)

A fisherman surfcasting from shore acted as if he didn't believe her that the boys were in danger. But a neighbor, Steve Robinson, who was also fishing from the Point, did, and after bellowing out to alert a nearby skiff, he jumped into the Bay and swam toward the kids. He later told a reporter the waves had become so high that once in the water he couldn't even see the boys. He was a good swimmer, but it took all he had to reach them. When he did, they looked exhausted and happy to see him. They grabbed him and climbed on his back.

He tried to swim that way, but quickly realized they could all drown. He told them, "I can only take one at a time!" But they both hung on. He tried swimming as hard as he could but to no avail. Now convinced he couldn't do it, he decided to release the boys, telling them to try to keep their heads above the water, while he swam toward shore to get help. Almost there, he got caught in the vice grip of the current, stuck in one place, and began to drown.

Seeing Robinson go under, Sheridan plunged back into the water, immediately getting caught in the rip current. By then the Coast Guardsmen on duty had spotted the two boys through their binoculars and rushed to the shore to help. Yelling to Seaman Apprentice James Wallenschlager to grab life preservers, Duty Officer Andy Nichols dove into the surf. In less than a minute, he realized he couldn't reach the boys, and fought the current back to shore. Back on the sand, he threw Sheridan a foam cooler for flotation, while Wallenschlager tossed a life preserver to Robinson. Nelson had swallowed "a bellyful of water," he later recounted, "but all I could think about was the rescue." He ran back to the lighthouse and pulled out the canoe.

Seeing the nearer boy sinking under the water and gasping for breath, Robinson threw him the life preserver. Sheridan was clinging to the foam cooler, trying to catch her breath, all of her strength depleted, when everything suddenly appeared to move in slow motion.

"I thought I was going to die, and I wondered what would happen to my children," she said.

About an hour earlier, around the corner from the Robinsons' home, retiree George Parrish had left his cottage on Elm Drive to check his crab pots. He had two out in the cove, as permitted by the Department of Natural Resources. Just as he did several times a week, he drove his dark green pickup truck the two blocks to the beach, where he offloaded his six-horsepower Evinrude from the back and carried it, cradled in his arms, the 100 or so feet across the sand to his twelve-foot aluminum row boat, overturned beneath a cedar, above the high-water line. Then he returned to the truck for the red, two-gallon gas can. In minutes he was dragging the small boat down to the water's edge, his gear secured onboard. With the breeze blowing from the northeast, the waters on the south side of the Point were calm, allowing him to step in and shove off without difficulty. In another minute, he was out in the cove, pulling up the first pot.

Parrish had a bushel basket in the bow, just in case he was lucky, and by habit, two flotation seats, twice the legal requirement. The first pot (a two-by-two foot wire cube with whatever bait was handy that week fastened in the middle) was directly offshore about 200 feet. Finding it empty except for untouched fish-head bait, he headed steadily toward his next buoy, off Hemlock Drive, the last beach entrance before the sandbar at the Point. The Evinrude made just a low hum as he approached— not enough to drown out the cries for help rising from the other side of the bar. He quickly spotted one of the boys, treading water in the rolling waves. Then he spotted the second small head bobbing near the first. He turned up the throttle and headed around the Point. Nearing the boys, he tossed them the two flotation seats; then, carefully maneuvering the skiff, he pulled them one at a time up over the port side. Somehow—it was later all a blur— Sheridan and Robinson managed to get to shore, along with Nichols in the canoe.

When all were safely ashore, a Solomons Fire and Rescue ambulance summoned by Nichols examined the near-drowning victims and found only Nichols in need of medical treatment. He spent the next two days at the Navy hospital being treated for water in his lungs.

That weekend, a novice, twenty-two-year-old reporter for the *Calvert Recorder*, Yvonne Heffner, gathered together the drama's principal players, with the exception of George Parrish, to recount their near-death experience. They posed for a group photograph on the lighthouse beach, where it all began.

The two little boys were nine-year-old twins, Nick and Greg Fernando, who were visiting their grandfather at Cove Point Beach while their parents were in New York. They'd been wading knee-deep in the water along the sandbar when their footing gave way and they fell into the current that would sweep them out into the Bay.

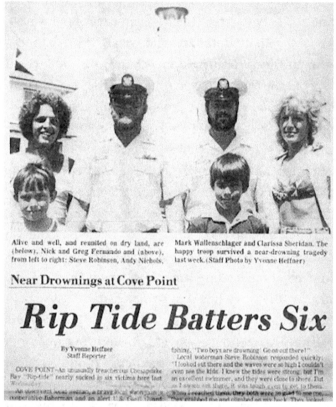

Alive and well, and reunited on dry land, are (below), Nick and Greg Fernando and (above), from left to right: Steve Robinson, Andy Nichols, Mark Wallenschlager and Clarissa Sheridan. The happy troop survived a near-drowning tragedy last week. (Staff Photo by Yvonne Heffner)

Near Drownings at Cove Point

Rip Tide Batters Six

By Yvonne Heffner
Staff Reporter

COVE POINT—An unusually treacherous Chesapeake Bay "Rip-tide" nearly sucked in six victims here last

fishing, "Two boys are drowning! Go on out there!"
Local waterman Steve Robinson responded quickly: "I looked out there and the waves were so high I couldn't even see the kids. I knew the tides were strong, but I'm an excellent swimmer, and they were close to shore. But as I swam out there, it was tough even to get to them.

Calvert Recorder front-page article on rescue at Cove Point.

Heffner's meticulously detailed report ran top-center on the front page. There's no telling how many other lives her story may have saved during the following weeks of that summer, or even the next. But newspapers are gone the next day. Memories fade; new folks, young and old, are drawn to a beach by the cool waters and soothing breezes. And some would not know about the devil below—for Cove Point Beach residents, right next door.

THE BROTHERS, JULY 24, 2015

Daniel and Doug Brown were like kids at the beach, stripping off their shirts as fast as they could and leaping into the Bay. Doug was thirty-nine and his brother thirty-seven, but to see them splashing and joking in the water with Dan's seventeen-year-old son, Jason, anyone would think they were all three teenagers. Dan's house was on Beach Drive, near the opposite end of the community and about midpoint in the cove. Why the men chose to swim at the Point, rather than in the cove, is not clear. It may have seemed more exciting if the breezes were from the northeast; maybe there just wasn't anyone else there at six o'clock on a warm Friday evening. Or it may have been the greater chance of finding shark teeth while beachcombing near the lighthouse. That's what Dan's girlfriend was doing.

Eventually, the waves started rolling in faster and the current began to pull at their legs. Their feet suddenly couldn't touch the bottom. Jason later told *The Washington Post* that the mood turned serious, Doug telling the others, "Let's get back." But when his uncle tried to paddle toward shore, he seemed to be on a treadmill, and he started to drift away. Jason recalled turning to his dad and asking if he was okay. He was not. All three started yelling to Dan's girlfriend on the beach, but she couldn't hear them over the sound of the surf. Jason told the *Post* he gripped his father's arms, but his 250-pound frame was too heavy to pull. Finally, Dan told his son to leave him. His last words before disappearing under the waves—"I love you." There was no sign of Doug.

Less than 100 yards from the beach, Ana Giordano and her husband, Shawn Carroll, were relaxing on their porch in the cool shade of a dozen or more tall pines. Carroll, celebrating the end of the workweek with a cold Corona, had just finished mowing the lawn, while Giordano meticulously weeded the flowerbeds. The only sounds at the dead-end of Calvert Boulevard, a stone's throw from the lighthouse, were the chirping of crickets and the loud "cheer...cheer... cheer" of a cardinal warning off an intruder. The couple was looking forward to a peaceful weekend.

Suddenly they heard other sounds, raucous, entirely out of sync with the serenity of the scene. At first, Carroll thought people were fighting, shouting angrily at each other. It wasn't until his wife heard it the third time that she leapt to her feet, blurting "someone's crying 'help!'" The couple raced toward the beach, taking a shortcut between two other houses. At first they saw no one. Then they spotted a woman walking above the high-water line near the lighthouse fence. They ran toward her, calling out, "What's going on?" When she realized they were referring to shouts they'd both heard, she waved a hand dismissively, saying, "Oh those guys! They're always teasing!"

But just then, all three spotted a skinny young man crawling, exhausted, out of the surf, "like a wet albatross." His face contorted with terror and pain, he shouted, "They're still out there!" Suddenly, the young woman panicked; it all came together. Her boyfriend and his brother were drowning.

Carroll ran to the nearest house where he knew he'd find a kayak. His next-door neighbor, Tim Whitehouse, who also had heard the cries for help, ran with him and helped carry the tandem craft to the water. But he could not paddle out with Carroll, Whitehouse quickly explained, because he couldn't swim.

Beyond the shore, Carroll found the sea kayak easy to maneuver. On the beach, several more people had gathered and were shouting to him, pointing to various objects bobbing in the water that they thought might be the swimmers. But each time, it turned out to be just another buoy, tethered to a crab pot on the Bay floor. Carroll kept paddling, scanning the water until the surface suddenly erupted in a turbulent chop beneath the tap-tap-tap of a rescue helicopter hovering overhead. There was nothing more he could do.

Meanwhile, Jason, unable to find any flotation device on the beach to aid the rescue attempt, ran back toward his father's house to get a boogie board. A cross-country runner, he sprinted as if his own life were at stake, all the while calling out for help.

A neighbor who heard his cry as he passed her house said she would never forget it as long as she lived.

At dark the search was called off. Dan's body was recovered the next day. Doug's was found by a search boat two days later, caught on a buoy above one of Bobby Darnell's crab pots, east of the lighthouse.

THE WATERMEN

If there was one resident of Cove Point Beach who knew more than anyone about the devil beneath the surface at the lighthouse beach, it was Bobby Darnell. His parents had a vacation home in the cove since before he was born, and the family lived on the Bay full-time since he was a teenager. He bought his own crab boat and built a successful business as soon as he'd graduated from Calvert High School in 1983.

Darnell's inspiration was a waterman named Julian Creighton, nicknamed "Buster," which also happened to be the name of his crab boat. Young Bobby was just five years old when he first spied Buster tending his pots a short distance off the beach. Sometimes the sun, a fiery ball, was barely peeking over the Eastern Shore as Buster emptied the crabs into bushel baskets. He'd quickly replenish the bait before dropping the traps back into fifteen feet of water. The deep putt-putt of the diesel engine as the craft glided from one buoy to the next was an unmistakable signal to sleeping beachfront families that the day was beginning. And following behind would be the inevitable "mewing" (as fishermen call it) of the seagulls tracking the boat's wake in hopes of snatching a stray scrap.

Besides his one or two helpers (often high schoolers in summer), the gulls were the waterman's only companions. Few other boats were anywhere in sight, especially on a weekday. On weekends, much farther out, charter boats with a dozen or more fishermen aboard would speed by en route to some of the best fishing on the Bay. Sometimes the scene was so beautiful, a little kid could hardly imagine anything better. That's when Bobby, at the age of five, found himself thinking, "That's what I want to do!"—a thought that never left him.

If he ever figured in those early days that a waterman's life would be easy, he was soon corrected. One October morning in 1979, Buster Creighton left his homeport at Hooper's Island, on the Eastern Shore, just after dawn as usual, to tend his crab pots off Cove Point. About 9 a.m., he suddenly fell over the side into the Bay. Bobby figures he must have slipped on something on deck, perhaps a sea nettle. He says it has happened to him, also sending him flying overboard. Buster's helper managed to grab his hand as the younger man struggled in the water, trying to remove his heavy boots before they filled with water. But both hands were slippery. To his would-be rescuer's horror, Buster slipped from his grip and was swept away, caught in the grasp of something stronger than either man. The thirty-three-year-old waterman drowned.

That morning, fourteen-year-old Bobby Darnell and his father were fishing near the Point in their small aluminum skiff while search boats dredged the waters for Buster's body. Unaware of what had happened, Bobby took pictures of the slow-moving vessels. He didn't learn of Buster's drowning until it was reported in the *Waterman's Gazette*, a monthly magazine that Bobby followed avidly.

Buster Creighton's accident was not Bobby's first encounter with tragedy on the Bay. Walking the beach one Saturday morning as a pre-teen, looking for a promising spot to cast his line, he was stopped in his tracks by a sickening odor. Just yards ahead in the surf lay the body of a man who'd drowned after falling from a sailboat. Adults who showed up quickly shooed Bobby away. It was the worst moment of his youth in a place described by generations of youngsters before and after as an almost magical place in space and time. These experiences would inform the future waterman's compass. He knew if he were to follow the life he admired so much, he had to learn where the devil lurked beneath the waters, and never underestimate its power.

THE INCONCEIVABLE, AUGUST 1, 2015

Like the Fernando twins three decades earlier, fifty-seven-year-old Michael Oliver wasn't even swimming. He didn't know how. Even if he did, he might not have tried because he knew about the fate of Dan and Doug Brown, the brothers who had drowned at that very beach near the Cove Point Lighthouse just eight days earlier. All Oliver was doing was wading in the water, less than waist deep, which happens to be the place where a rip current frequently captures its prey, sweeping the unaware off their feet and dragging them out to deep water.

His friend Tim Whitehouse, who just the week before had aided in the failed rescue of the Brown brothers, was beachcombing for fossils when he heard Oliver's screams. Another man on the beach tried to reach him, but failed. Other volunteers with boogie boards and a life ring ran into the water, attempting to find him.

Bobby Darnell was tending his pots a couple of hundred yards off the much broader hollow that forms Cove Point Beach. Well-acquainted with the rip current on the north side of the sandbar, he only worked in those waters on an outgoing tide. When the tide was incoming, he explained, the rip current pushed his boat due east with a force so strong it was impossible to tend the traps. The water entering the tiny hollow between the lighthouse and the sandbar has to go somewhere. And that somewhere is straight out, creating the strongest rip current he had encountered anywhere on the estuary.

A woman in a kayak paddled frantically toward Darnell's crab boat as he emptied his traps, chasing him as fast as she could as he glided from one to the next. Suddenly he realized she was yelling something. Someone was drowning, he finally heard, as she pointed back toward the lighthouse. Darnell turned his forty-foot vessel toward the area north of the sandbar (which locals call the Point). There were several people in the water on boogie boards, but one young couple, clinging to a white life ring, appeared to be in distress, struggling against the current that was dragging them farther out into the Bay. Darnell assumed they were the reason for the kayaker's plea and the onlookers pointing excitedly from the beach. He slowed his 220-horsepower diesel to a gentle throttle, pulled alongside the two, a man and woman appearing to be in their mid-twenties, and hauled them into the boat. No sooner aboard, they breathlessly pointed back to the water. Someone was drowning, they panted. That's why they had ventured out, using the life ring from the lighthouse, to try to find him.

The waterman turned his attention back to the low but persistent waves some 200 feet from shore, squinting to distinguish anything in the water besides the white buoys tethered to his own crab pots. Suddenly he spotted the victim, a man appearing to be short of stature, with long hair, looking almost like a boy, floating face down near one of the buoys. Darnell turned the boat toward him, while motioning to a Solomons Rescue Squad team arriving on the scene to head in the same direction. The rescue boat got to the buoy first and pulled the victim aboard. They thought they detected a pulse, although Oliver had been in the water at least thirty minutes. The boat raced back to the waiting ambulance onshore. But it was too late; Oliver was declared dead upon arrival at Calvert Memorial Hospital.

Within days, multiple signs were posted warning against entering the water on the lighthouse side of the Point, due to the life-threatening rip current.

Rip current warning signs on Cove Point Beach and near the Lighthouse. (Courtesy Carol Booker)

Tending his traps near the Point, Bobby Darnell gets mad when he sees beachgoers, often with children, entering the waters between the Cove Point Lighthouse and the sandbar, sometimes wading, looking for shark teeth; sometimes plunging in for a swim. Perhaps they haven't noticed the signs; maybe they've ignored them; or maybe they just don't "get it." He knows that someday, the devil will again be waiting.

11

BEHEMOTHS ON THE BAY

The only road out ran past the gas plant.

If Cook Webster had any vision for the future of the
virgin timberland and freshwater marsh abutting his
"Atlantic City on the Bay" at Cove Point, it's unlikely
to have included a liquid natural gas terminal. But
that's exactly what arrived some four decades after
his death, in 1938. His beach resort as well as all of
Maryland had very mixed feelings about it.

The vision that stunned many when his heirs
signed a deed conveying more than 1,000 acres of
extraordinary Bayside for use as a gas importation
terminal was one of desecration: towering holding
tanks; ugly pipelines; and a multi-legged behemoth
rising out of the pristine waters of the Chesapeake,
all of it in shocking contrast to the natural, mystic
beauty of 100-foot tall cliffs and virgin wetlands.
Others saw undreamed of tax dollars flowing into
this rural county.

The deal with Columbia Liquid Natural Gas Corp.
closed on April 3, 1971, three months after the
Glascocks declared done and over with their earlier
deals with two different mining companies that,
for a short time, had turned the shoreline into an
industrial eyesore. Of further concern to many in the

Cove Point vicinity was the proximity of the proposed gas terminal to another newcomer—a nuclear power plant—under construction just three miles up the Bay. That reality triggered frightful visions of what could happen. But the gas plant alone, even without the nearby nuclear plant, was enough to scare the barnacles off some of the crustiest neighbors. Those old enough to remember pointed to the liquid natural gas storage plant explosions in Cleveland in 1944, which resulted in the most devastating fire in the city's history, killing more than 120 persons in a fifty-block area.

Loudspeakers blaring "Get out! The neighborhood is on fire! Run eastward!" had sent people wading into Lake Erie to escape sheets of flame. Residents of Cove Point Beach wondered how they could escape such a catastrophe by land given that the only road out of the community ran past the proposed plant. Water escapes using the small rowboats and kayaks a few residents kept on the beach were out of the question. No comfort was taken in the East Ohio Gas Company's admission in 1944 that they were "completely at a loss" concerning the cause of the blasts.

Project promoters remained confident: *That was almost thirty years ago. The industry is safer now, more regulated. It couldn't happen here—or at least it's unlikely.*

The greatest opposition came from conservationists. The Sierra Club and the Maryland Conservation Council pointed out the threats to unique scenic,

MANY DIE, 200 HURT IN CLEVELAND FIRE

Huge Tanks at East Side Gas Plant Explode and Flames Strike 50-Block Area

---

PANIC IS WIDESPREAD

Dead at 28 and May Reach 40 —City's Record Blaze Is Out of Control for Hours

---

CLEVELAND, Saturday, Oct. 21 (*P*)—Thunderous explosions ripped a $6,000,000 liquid gas storage plant yesterday afternoon and spread the most devastating fire in Cleveland's history over a 50-block East Side area, causing many deaths and injury to at least 200.

AP article: Many die, 200 hurt.

esthetic, educational, and recreational characteristics, in an area that had been designated for a state park. It included one of the few remaining public beaches on the Bay, as well as a scenic marsh frequented by swans, migrating ducks, turtles and a host of botanical beauties. Columbia, they charged, didn't need all 1,100 acres, and could have chosen any of several more appropriate and available industrial sites—in Anne Arundel County, for instance, or at Baltimore's harbor. In fact, the Federal Power Commission itself, whose approval of the site was necessary, should have sought alternative sites.

Two things seemed certain: the legal battle would be lengthy, and the outcome unpredictable. Given those two factors, both sides agreed to a settlement. Instead of running a more than mile-long pipeline out over the surface of the Bay to a huge, two-berth loading platform, the pipeline would be buried in a tunnel the entire distance. The majority of the property not used for the terminal—about 600 acres—would be protected by a conservation easement. The 190-acre marsh would be preserved in its natural form. Also in the settlement was Columbia's agreement to lease twenty-five acres as open space to the Cove Point Beach Association for recreation purposes, and to convey that parcel to the association or to the state of Maryland if the company ever decided to dispose of it.

The final agreement, an easement rather than a lease, assured the association's members exclusive access to the beach north of the lighthouse, with its magnificent view of the Bay, uninterrupted by anything but the towering monster pier a mile offshore.

WHITE DUST

In April 1974, a joint venture of two out-of-state companies was awarded the contract to construct the offshore, 2,500-foot pier, along with the tube-tunnel to house the pipelines that would bring the liquefied natural gas to the shore and the plant.

The jobs that came with the project were considered a major plus for the county, although many of the workers came from surrounding counties and even other states. When construction was finished, the plant itself was expected to employ about 200 at peak.

Some of the construction jobs came with a high price for workers, which they would confront years later. One of those workers was Roy Hayes, who had earlier worked on the Calvert Cliffs Nuclear Power Plant construction, his first job in Calvert County. That was around 1973, when he was in his early twenties. He was a member of Local 24 of the International Association of Heat and Frost Insulators. He recalls that they were called "asbestos workers" at first, and "insulators" when asbestos became controversial and its use restricted. Their job began after steamfitters and others had done their part in the construction of the plant.

His closest call—and worst experience—at Calvert Cliffs came after the plant was up and running, when he was doing general maintenance. He was working alone on the insulation of a pipe when the heat became unbearable. Feeling as if he might become ill, he headed to a cool-down area, where he passed out from heat exhaustion. When he awoke, he was on a stretcher, being carried to an ambulance for transport to Calvert Memorial Hospital, where he was found to be just a couple of degrees shy of heat stroke. Ironically, he says, it was snowing as the ambulance raced toward the hospital.

Hayes and his coworkers were always aware that the heat in areas of the plant was a potentially lethal hazard. What they did not know was that right from the outset, when they participated in its construction, there had been another, more pervasive threat to their lives in plain view.

Hayes and his crew wore street clothes, which he remembers were covered in "white dust" at the end of their shift, as was everything else. The blocks of Unibestos they were strapping together to insulate mechanical equipment gave off air-borne particles containing asbestos. (Unibestos insulations had higher than average asbestos content, and when the manufacturer, Pittsburgh Corning Corp., filed for bankruptcy in 2000, it was facing tens of thousands of lawsuits from people with asbestos-related diseases.)

"We'd be pure white from it," Hayes recalls. Although surgical type masks were available, he says most of the workers didn't wear them. Hayes was among those who found it difficult to breathe wearing the mask.

Since there were no showers at the plant for the workers, Hayes drove home to Prince George's County "covered in the dust," unwittingly exposing his whole family to the fibers on his clothing, hair, skin and shoes. Years later, when his job was the removal of asbestos, the crews were required to wear a full-face mask and suit. But for Hayes and others it was too late.

When construction of the gas plant started, about a year later, he recalls that many people were concerned about how near it was—about three miles —to the nuclear power plant. He wasn't so much concerned as surprised at this proximity.

Working for a subcontractor, Hayes' job was to insulate the tunnel running under the Bay from the holding tanks to the offshore platform. That task was particularly challenging when the Bay froze over during the extraordinary deep freeze of February 1977, the coldest winter in 200 years. But like the heat he'd faced in the nuclear power plant, the ice in the Bay wasn't the greatest threat. Hayes and coworkers would not know until decades later that the greatest threat they faced was from the materials they were using in the confined space.

By this time, the insulating material was a kind of foam encased in fiberglass, rather than the asbestos they had used at the nuclear plant. After the crew chemically welded the pieces of insulation together, they cleaned their hands and tools with methylene chloride (also known as DCM), a solvent used in a range of products, such as paint strippers. DCM has been linked to cancer, cognitive impairment, and asphyxiation. Exposure can also lead to a heart attack.

In 2013, the U.S. Occupational Safety and Health Administration and the National Institute for Occupational Safety and Health reported that more than a dozen bathtub refinishers had died after working with DCM in poorly ventilated areas.

Hayes recalls that at least two men working in the confined spaces in the tunnel died suddenly, but doesn't recall any mention of the deaths in the press. Another worker who had had a particularly concentrated exposure to DCM died of a heart attack. Two others died driving home from work, but their deaths were attributed to alcohol, although he believes that the presence of DCM in their systems may have contributed to disorientation or confusion. In 2019, the U.S. Environmental Protection Agency banned the manufacture, import, processing and sale of methylene chloride in all paint removers for consumer use.

Today, retired and living in Calvert County, Hayes has asbestosis, a respiratory disease caused by inhalation of asbestos fibers which cause permanent, irreversible scarring of the lungs. He says he could not prove which of his exposures to the toxin caused the damage. Signs of the disease, like those of mesothelioma, also related to asbestos exposure, often do not appear until decades after first exposure. Hayes knows of other men with whom he worked who have died of mesothelioma.

SHIP AHOY!

On February 25, 1978, a *Baltimore Sun* editorial, headlined "LNG Safety," cited the safety record at eighty-nine LNG facilities around the country, where there had been no major accidents since safeguards were adopted following the 1944 Cleveland disaster. The editorial writer acknowledged, however, that these other facilities were small, unlike the one at Cove Point, which would soon start receiving "huge" shipments of LNG via special tankers. The paper noted that Congress's Office of Technology Assessment had warned of deficiencies in federal-state inspection protocols and that those "gaps" had not yet been filled. On the positive side, the editorial continued:

> *At least one of OTA's caveats already has*
> *been heeded: The terminal was placed in*
> *a rural rather than a populated area.*

Opponents of the plant pointed out that Columbia had understated the size of the surrounding population. In any case, for residents of Cove Point, that "rural" area was their home, and the gas terminal's presence in their backyard was cause for concern.

On March 13, 1978, the first tanker loaded with Algerian gas nudged up to the new dock off Cove Point, the culmination of negotiations that had begun in 1970. Other vessels, described by the *Baltimore Sun* as "huge double-hulled ships built like giant thermos bottles" would soon follow on a regular basis.

In January 1979, a *Sun* editorial was almost euphoric in its conclusions regarding the Cove Point terminal's bright future. After touting the imported gas prices as "reasonable by today's standards" because "contracts for the LNG were negotiated with the Algerians some years ago," the commentary dismissed charges that Algeria was "an unreliable supplier." The newspaper's reasoning was that Algeria had "a huge investment in its gas liquefaction facilities and only a limited number of customers equipped to receive the LNG."

The editorial dismissed charges that the operation was unsafe, citing two studies that it said concluded that "the chance of a repetition of the Cleveland disaster is almost nil." It also quoted Columbia as saying it had paid "strict attention to implementing" widely available technologies for safe handling of LNG at its terminal. The Office of Technology Assessment, it went on to say, was "not quite as sanguine about terminal safety" but agreed that "the newer terminals seem relatively risk free."

The editorial concluded optimistically:

> *The Cove Point facility seems destined to become an important part of the Maryland economy—one from which can be expected safe operation and a permanent contribution to employment and the tax base.*

Two-hundred-eighty-six days later, on October 6, 1979, the Cove Point LNG plant was the site of the worst LNG explosion since the Cleveland conflagration thirty-five years earlier. And just six months after that, on April 1, 1980, Algeria suspended shipments to the U.S. because it considered the price too low. A month later, the North African country announced it was ceasing development and exportation of liquid natural gas entirely, leading to multimillion dollar annual losses for Columbia and its partner, Consolidated Gas, over the next 10 years.

EXPLOSION

U.S. Rep. Edward Markey, whose Massachusetts district included a liquid natural gas plant in Boston harbor, inspected the Cove Point plant after the explosion in preparation for Congressional hearings on LNG safety. Speaking with reporters, he asked, "Do you know how much gas it took for that explosion? It took one gallon."

"And," he added, "the storage plant holds 1.3 billion gallons."

The explosion occurred around 3:30 a.m. A faulty seal on one of ten pumps at a terminal building had allowed liquefied gas, kept at minus 260 degrees Fahrenheit, to seep out into a conduit carrying electrical wires. The conduit ran underground a couple hundred feet to a main electrical station, warming along the way and finally filling a room with colorless, odorless vapor. Henry Hunter, 30, of Lexington Park, Maryland, was making his routine, night-shift rounds when he noticed a telltale frost caused by the liquid gas on the connecting box. He radioed his supervisor, Charles Bromley, 31, also from Lexington Park. The two men then went to the electrical station to cut off power to the leaking pump as a safety precaution. They entered the station, unaware of the concentration of escaped gas, and Hunter threw the circuit breaker to disconnect the pump. That action caused a spark, igniting the gas, which then exploded, killing Bromley, badly injuring Hunter, and destroying the cinderblock building, about the size of a two-car garage.

The Maryland Occupational Safety and Health Advisory Board charged Columbia with "serious and willful" violations at the terminal. The company appealed, arguing that they were in full compliance with federal regulations, a point conceded by federal regulators who accepted part of the blame. Nevertheless, after a six-month investigation, the National Transportation Safety Board cited the terminal operator for failure to install an alarm system sensitive enough to warn workers of potentially explosive leaks, failure to install a backup seal near the place where the leak occurred, and failure to have spark-proof electrical equipment—any one of which might have prevented the fatal explosion. The report concluded that no safety analysis was made or required during planning, design, or construction of the Cove Point terminal. The problem of the failed pump seal, the Safety Board concluded, "could have been detected during the design of the LNG facility through the application of the most basic safety analysis techniques."

SUPPLY AND DEMAND

The terminal was back in operation two weeks after the deadly October 6 blast, and by the end of October 1979, tankers were once again delivering gas to the pier. The industry, however, was undergoing a vast change. The scarcity that led to protracted negotiations with a foreign supplier had now turned to glut.

Shortly after the first tanker arrived at Cove Point, the U.S. began deregulating natural gas, making new drilling more profitable than before. Suddenly the U.S. had a gas bubble of more natural gas than it could use. Now the Energy Department was treating it as a preferred fuel and encouraging its use, a turnaround from its earlier policy of conservation and prohibition of new customers.

Algeria, meanwhile, had been pressing for higher prices. An amended contract kept deliveries coming until April 1980, when the Algerian government cut them off. Staffing at the Cove Point terminal shrank from 125 to thirty-seven employees. The plant would continue to store gas onsite to meet periodic shortages. But activity on the grounds was hardly noticeable. The press called it Cove Point's "Ghost Terminal." And that's when, as far as the area's watermen were concerned, the fun began.

For the next twenty years, the hottest fishing hole in the middle Chesapeake was under and around the idle terminal. By the time the tankers stopped coming, the massive pilings had grown encrusted with barnacles and vegetation, luring small fish to feed, and larger ones to take advantage of their distraction. The bounty for anglers included striped bass (rockfish), bluefish, red drum, perch, spot and occasional surprises. Rules banning fishing near the pilings were rarely if ever enforced.

On shore, Cove Pointers could walk north for miles searching for fossils, stopping at the marsh to catch a glimpse of its tranquil beauty, even climbing up and over Columbia's small pier running into the Bay opposite the offshore docking/loading platform. No one ever objected. The beachcombers could wander on until felled trees or a high tide blocked further passage toward Rocky Point and Calvert Cliffs State Park. Most of the time, one could do so without ever encountering another human.

12

THE EVIL WITHIN

I will always love you

There was nothing particularly "collectible" in Mark Kahl's knife collection, but an invitation to view it was enough to pique a young boy's interest. And that was what Kahl wanted. He also kept other "curiosities" at the house. Two lively ferrets, one black and white, and the other taupe and black, romped in cages in the carport. He said he'd named them Ricky and Andrew, which just happened to be the names of two of the three neighborhood boys he'd invited to see the knives one Saturday morning during the summer of 1996.

The boys, both thirteen, were already somewhat suspicious of the strawberry blond man living in the bungalow between Lighthouse Boulevard and the wetlands. It wasn't anything about the house or even the abandoned yellow school bus behind it, used for storage, that "creeped" them out. They didn't know the exact age of the slight man—5'8" and 135 pounds—but his interest in hanging out with them seemed odd. Without ever putting their suspicions into words, Ricky and their younger sidekick, twelve-year-old Zach, had already agreed that if Kahl "ever tried anything," they "could take him."

He told them the ferrets were rescues he'd acquired in his work as an assistant at the veterinary practice up the road in Prince Frederick. It was all a lie. Two small dogs, a Pekingese and a border collie mix, were the only other creatures living with him full time. But he would sometimes have a cherubic-faced young boy, about thirteen years old, staying over on weekends that summer. The boy shyly told anyone who asked that Kahl was his "uncle," looking uneasy as he said it. If asked, he also said he lived across the Patuxent River, in St. Mary's County.

Little Zach recalled that the visitor was eager to play with the Cove Point kids. He had a bike, apparently new, and would plead with them not to go home just yet at dinnertime, but to keep racing up and down Lighthouse Boulevard one more time. In fact, Zach recalled later, the boy always seemed reluctant to return to Kahl's house at the end of the day, but never said why.

Sometime in late fall 1996, Kahl's "nephew" stopped coming. The Cove Point kids hardly noticed, since the visitor's weekends at the beach had always been sporadic. Besides, only about a third, at most, of the property owners at Cove Point Beach were full-timers, and by November many of the summer people had already closed up their cottages for the winter.

Over in St. Mary's, the truth was coming out. The thirteen-year-old and his brother, a year older, had told their mother they were avoiding Kahl, the manager of the apartment complex the family moved into in 1995. Kahl had befriended her sons, acting like a big brother to them. He was especially attentive to the younger one, then just twelve, giving him odd jobs to do and paying him with little gifts. After winning the mother's trust, he'd started inviting the brothers to stay with him for summer weekends at his home in Cove Point Beach. The way he described it sounded like free summer camp. She agreed. The kids at Cove Point only remembered meeting one of the boys, the younger one.

Now, the brothers showed their mother letters, described as "love letters," Kahl had written to the younger boy when he stopped accepting his invitations to the beach, pleading with the child to see him again. The mother confronted Kahl and said she was contacting the police. Almost immediately, another letter to the thirteen-year-old appeared in the mailbox. She opened it, and what she read brought a flood of anger and pain such as she'd never experienced before. It was an explicit, four-page, love letter. "I will always love you, need you and care about you no matter whether you are 13 years old or 103 years old," it stated.

> *You'll be my son to me. Please don't give a young 'old man' an ulcer or heart attack. Let me know you're OK and that you still care. I worry about you every day.*

At times both flattering and seductive, the letter continued with offers of gifts, including designer clothing. It mentioned the dirt bike Kahl had bought that summer. The mother turned it over to the police, along with other letters. State troopers from Leonardtown and Prince Frederick interviewed both boys. On February 6, 1997, Maryland State Police arrested Kahl, thirty-five, and soon he was facing charges of second and third degree sex offense and two counts of child abuse.

The *Calvert Recorder* ran the news on its front page, under a one-column head: "Child molestation charges filed." Zach's mother saw it, and immediately called Ricky and Andrew's mothers. Both were shocked. None of the boys had ever shared their concerns about Kahl with a parent.

Kahl posted a $25,000 bond and was released the next day. In June, he pleaded guilty to second and third degree sex offenses against both brothers at his Cove Point home. He had been convicted in 1989 in Los Angeles of sexual abuse of young boys. His attorney told the judge Kahl was a diagnosed pedophile. He was sentenced to twenty years in prison.

After serving thirteen years, Kahl was paroled in January 2011. But his freedom was short-lived. One of the conditions of his parole was submission to periodic polygraph testing. In April 2011, just three months after his release, he admitted during the test that he had recently viewed child pornography. A subsequent examination of his computer confirmed that he had downloaded ten images and had searched the Internet for child pornography. His parole was revoked and he was returned to prison to serve the remaining seven years of his Maryland sentence plus fifteen years, to run concurrently, on the child pornography charge, followed by supervised release for life.

In the beauty and tranquility of the Cove, most residents never knew the danger had existed. The fondest memories of most long-time residents invoke their own freedom as children, or that of their children, to ride bicycles, roam the beach, and explore the forests with no greater worry than an occasional patch of poison ivy, as long as they didn't swim at the Point. It just wasn't the sort of community where "don't take candy from strangers" was considered a necessary warning.

13

THE GIANT AWAKENS

How beautiful is night!
a dewey freshness fills the silent air

—Robert Southey, 1829

British poet Robert Southey could have been sitting on the beach beneath the Cove Point Lighthouse when he penned those words, just one year after the light's installation. But almost two centuries later, he may have thought differently. By 2018, an irritating groan would have smothered the silence when a humongous LNG tanker was filling up at the gas plant's offshore platform.

The awakening of the sleeping giant in the Chesapeake north of the Cove Point Lighthouse was slow, fitful, and ultimately disappointing to fishermen, who were once again shooed away from the off-shore pier (long dubbed the "fish factory") by Coast Guard vessels, even when a tanker was nowhere in sight. After being dormant for almost two decades, the Columbia Liquid Natural Gas tanks towering over the marsh were reopened in 1995 as a storage site for energy companies in peak winter months. But the facility still looked somnambulant to passersby. In 2000, Columbia finally gave up, selling the entire operation. The buyer soon had problems as well, and in 2002 sold the terminal to Dominion Energy Inc., a Richmond-based power and energy company that sold natural gas around the country, as far west as Utah.

By the following year, renovations of the terminal and refurbishing of the offshore platform were underway in anticipation of welcoming the first tanker full of foreign liquid natural gas that summer. Gas supplies across the country were the tightest in decades, and prices—up more than 70 percent in the last year—were high enough to make Dominion's reported expenditure of $180 million to refurbish the facility well worth it. By 2005, the terminal would welcome eighty tankers as other energy companies talked about constructing import facilities. But by 2012, the market had again changed radically. The demand for foreign gas was down; just one ship off-loaded at the Cove Point terminal that year, and only two in 2013, to the delight of local watermen.

Calvert County officials were not as pleased. The loss of the plant, which was paying the county $15 million annually in property taxes, as well as employing about 100 workers, meant trouble for the county. With a mutual interest in saving the facility, the company and the county put their heads together to figure out a way forward. In 2013 they found it. The county offered a new tax deal while the company sought buyers for long-term domestic gas exports. Those deals would help pay for conversion of the plant into an export facility. Critics said the county's tax deal was too generous, and that Dominion would not have pulled out if Calvert, rather than offering a deal that included a forty-two percent tax reduction for nine years, had taken a tougher stand.

The Sierra Club, whose legal challenge against the original plant had ended in a settlement agreement in 1972, went back to court. The environmentalists argued that the agreement, as amended with Dominion in 2005, did not permit the proposed conversion of the terminal into an export facility. Allowing Dominion to convert the terminal to an export facility, they said, would not only damage the local environment but also contribute to global warming by supporting the fracking industry. They lost. The court interpreted the phrase "delivery by pipeline" to include a pipeline to a tanker waiting at the dock.

Cove Point residents watch as the tanker *Arctic Discoverer*, guided by tugs, passes the sandbar as it approaches Dominion's off-shore platform in 2016. The Bahamas flagged vessel has a capacity of 139,759 cubic meters of liquid gas. (Courtesy Carol Booker)

By the time construction of the converted facility was completed in 2018, Maryland Governor Larry

Hogan had signed into law a ban on fracking, making the presence of a huge export terminal in the same state seem a glaring contradiction. Some Cove Pointers moved away out of concerns over the possibility of an explosion, or the level of greenhouse gas emissions, three times more than before exports began—but according to state officials, well within allowable limits. Many others just ignored it or took a philosophical view. As one older resident put it, "At 81, I have one foot in the grave anyway. I'm not afraid of the gas."

For residents of more than 265 homes, including all of those in Cove Point Beach and Cove of Calvert, the evacuation route in the event of an explosion at the facility would be toward rather than away from the plant. In response to that, Dominion in 2014 purchased a residential property on the south side of Cove Point Road, about a couple of hundred yards before the plant entrance, as a potential detour for evacuees from Cove Point. At the entrance to that property, a driveway leading into the community of Cove Point Woods, they erected a seven-foot tall, locked wooden gate with a sign reading "EMERGENCY USE ONLY."

Watchdogs saw the purchase as an admission that an explosion at the plant that would block the Cove Point evacuation route was a possibility. According to Dominion, if there were such an emergency, a plant security guard would unlock the gate for the evacuation of Cove Pointers. People would proceed

Locked gate to potential Dominion LNG evacuation route detour for evacuees from Cove Point. The route from the gate is through the community of Cove Point Woods (below).

Escape route: (Courtesy Carol Booker)

down a narrow driveway into the small community of Cove Point Woods, and from there, along with those residents, out to a two-lane artery leading south away from the plant. There is no mention of this detour on published maps of the emergency evacuation route. The plant's executive offices would be unaffected in any event: They are located off-site, in the Patuxent Business Park, about two miles away.

AN UNCERTAIN FUTURE

In July 2020 came the surprise announcement that Warren Buffet's Berkshire Hathaway Energy was buying Dominion's liquid natural gas transmission assets, including twenty-five percent of the Cove Point terminal. The announcement said Berkshire Hathaway would henceforth run the operation and Dominion was turning its focus to renewable energy.

Some observers saw the deal as a mistake for Buffet at a time when many utilities are switching from coal-generated power straight to renewable sources of energy, bypassing natural gas as a so-called "bridge fuel."

The debate suggests that the future of the Cove Point plant is as unpredictable today as at any time in the last forty-plus years. As one old-timer put it, "When the titanium mine closed, we thought we had the Point back. Then the gas plant came and we were pushed aside again until the tankers stopped coming. Then they came back and who knows what's next?

I'd just like to have the nights as quiet as before, without thinking I've forgotten to change my hearing aid batteries."

14

THEN AND NOW

What's past is prologue.
—Shakespeare, *The Tempest*

"Some things never change." Those words could be the theme of Cove Point Beach. In the almost ninety years since Cook Webster placed his exclamatory ads in Washington newspapers, many things about the crescent shaped, white sand beach, the bank-run gravel roads, the wooded lots, and single-family homes (many of them original to the early years) have remained the same. And some of the happenings go back eons.

The prehistoric horseshoe crab still crawls ashore from one end of the cove to the other in late May to mate and lay eggs. Now, as ever before, the peak usually coincides with a new or full moon. Come sunrise, early morning beach walkers will find large clusters of greenish eggs in the sand near the high-water mark. There will also be a half-dozen or so of the creatures, rolled on their backs by the receding surf, unable to return to the water without help, which is frequently given.

Offshore, the cownose rays will also have arrived by early June for the same purpose. If a fisherman surfcasting from the shore is distracted for a moment, one of these winged swimmers is likely to yank his rod from the sand spike and drag it into the Bay before he can grab it. If he does regain the rod and manages to reel in the ray (only after quite a fight), he'd better be careful to avoid its stinger. At least one resident didn't, and discovered he had something in common with Capt. John Smith. When the strange looking creature, pulled from the Bay, stung the 17th century explorer with the spike beneath its slender tail, he thought he was about to die. The pain of the sting was so extreme, he directed his crew to dig his grave.

The modern-day victim implored his wife to drive him as fast as possible to Calvert Memorial Hospital, twenty miles up the road in Prince Frederick, in search of an antidote. The emergency room staff told him they had none. The couple then raced farther north to a hospital in Prince George's County where they heard the same bad news. However, as evening approached, the fisherman's thoughts, like Capt. Smith's, turned in another direction, and it wasn't the grave. A gnawing in his stomach greater than the waning pain in his limb signaled it was time to eat rather than to die. It was dinnertime, and on both tables, the "enemy" was the main course. (Stingray venom is rarely deadly, unless it strikes the heart or abdomen; but try to convince someone writhing in pain.)

As in the days when Senator Webster's catches off Cove Point led the *Post's* fishing columns, the seasonal runs of bluefish, striped bass, Spanish mackerel, and occasional surprises such as red drum remain plentiful. There have been some lean years in between, especially for the striped bass, known locally as rockfish (Maryland's state fish), and regulations remain in place to protect its comeback. The 200-foot fishing pier near Park Drive is long gone. No one alive today recalls seeing it or even knows the year it disappeared.

The nights are another story. Once among the quietest places on the Bay, miles from a bridge, a highway, or even a marina, Cove Point was like an amphitheater. On a still autumn evening, a dog walker could hear the symphony of migratory waterfowl settling in for the night on the sheltered freshwater marsh. Today, that's a hit-or-miss proposition. When it's busy feeding a tanker, the gas plant's grinding cacophony drowns out the gadwalls and geese along with every other pleasant sound of the night.

Cove Point waterman Bobby Darnell empties his crab traps near the Lighthouse. (Photo by Jacob Briggs.)

At sunrise, the low murmur of a diesel-powered crab boat signals reveille as it cruises east and west across the Cove, pulling up traps, emptying the catch, replacing the bait. The captain steering between the rows of buoys is most likely Cove Point's resident waterman, still harvesting the blue-clawed delicacies after some forty years.

About thirty percent of property owners—a multi-racial population—are full-time residents, many of them retirees, a figure that has not changed much over at least the past forty years. A fair number of the part-timers, just as Sen. Webster envisioned, live and work in Washington, D.C., spending weekends and vacations at the beach.

A small change in recent years has been the appearance of a handful of Airbnbs, short-term rentals arranged over the Internet. The Cove Point Lighthouse, turned over to the County in 2000 to be managed by the Calvert Marine Museum, now offers the former keeper's and assistant keeper's residences—a two-and-a-half-story duplex—for short-term vacation stays.

THE ROADS

After decades of lobbying by the Cove Point Beach Association, the County finally installed speed bumps on Lighthouse Boulevard, the main artery and only paved road, to help enforce the 25-mph speed limit. Meanwhile, on the private, community-owned gravel roads, a sudden proliferation of golf carts has added to the resort atmosphere of the tiny community. A few years earlier, a survey of members confirmed a continuing preference for retaining the original, bank-run gravel, rather than any other resurfacing, preserving the community's country ambiance.

Calvert Boulevard, one of the community's gravel roads. (Courtesy Carol Booker)

THE RISING SEA

Although long-time residents of Cove Point Beach are likely to tell you that not much has changed in the decades they have lived here, the world beyond the colony's 1,100 acres has changed greatly. Some of those changes have affected the community or may in the future. Among the concerns are the possibility of a catastrophic event at the nuclear power plant a few miles away, or at the country's second largest liquid natural gas export facility next door. For many, the bigger issues are global warming and rising sea levels. Even some who don't accept greenhouse gases as a cause of the water in their yards are nevertheless concerned about it.

In 2014, Calvert County adopted a flood-mitigation plan for Cove Point, after identifying it as the county's most flood prone community, with eighty-five percent of its structures vulnerable to flooding and property damage.

Hurricane Isabel in September 2003, among the worst to hit eastern Maryland in at least seven decades, caused a storm surge of five to nine feet above normal tide, inundating the community. The impact was devastating, with most of Cove Point under water.

Homeowners, who had evacuated the day before, returned on foot through knee-high water on the main road.

Lighthouse Boulevard under water, Sept. 2003. (Courtesy Francis Brannan)

Brannan home flooded. (Courtesy Francis Brannan)

The Brannan family beach house on Holly Drive, their summer oasis since the early '50s, was one of many swamped by rising ground water.

Like most of the community's small bungalows built between the 1930s and '60s, it had a minimal foundation, adding to its vulnerability.

The water damage was so extensive, demolition was the only logical remedy. The Solomons Island Volunteer Rescue Squad and Fire Department took care of that.

Brannan home in flames: (Courtesy Francis Brannan)

The family decided to replace the cottage with a year-round home.

The county's flood-mitigation plan warned that hurricanes and severe storms were not the only dangers to the fragile community, built on a sand spit between the Bay and the marsh. Heavy rains and astronomical tides cause the water level to rise in the wetlands, referred to in the plan as a "shallow bay," flooding nearby properties and the main road.

Most scientists agree that the major reason for the rising sea level is humankind's insistence on burning fossil fuels that lessen the earth's protection from the heat of the sun, thus melting the ice caps. At Cove Point, the effect is manifested by a growing number of lots that fail to "perc" due to water saturation, rendering them unfit for traditional septic systems. When septic systems have failed in recent years, the community has seen the installation of new mound systems and bottomless sand filters, coupled with large, green nitrogen filter boxes and, as a last resort, septic holding tanks that require frequent pumping out. The possibility of public water and sewer being brought to the Point has been discussed with no resolution.

The entire community lies in a state-designated Critical Area—within 1000 feet of the Chesapeake Bay—requiring permits for most construction activities, as well as land-clearing. While some property owners grouse at the restraints, others applaud efforts to save the Bay.

IN THE MEANTIME …

Cove Point is a place between: midway between the headwaters and the mouth of the Chesapeake Bay, flanked to its north and south by fossil-laden cliffs that confirm its distinct place in time; a place between a prehistoric sea and a modern-day estuary that scientists say it is likely to sink beneath. The actions of humans will determine how soon. The county's flood-mitigation plan, by including projections into the next century, at least suggests hope that there may be some time.

The renovation of summer cottages, the building of year-round homes, the elevation of older structures to a level safe from flooding, the addition of solar panels (albeit gradually), and installation of at least one geothermal heating system—these are all signs of a community both serious and optimistic about the future.

Perhaps it's the mystic beauty of this place between heaven and earth. Or it may simply be the soothing legend of Tryn Trava, still lingering in the night air.

"Don't worry!" it whispers. And on most days, Cove Pointers just don't.

THE END

NOTES

CHAPTER 1.
THROUGH THE EXPLORER'S EYES

page nos.

5 The lean man with bushy beard: "A Calvert Hermit," *Baltimore Sun*, Oct. 15, 1896, p.7.

10 "There are few places that exceed this": ad in the *Maryland Gazette*, May 13, 1790, p.2.

CHAPTER 2. THE BEACON

13 steamboat *Georgia*: *Baltimore Sun*, Jan. 8, 1842, p.2.

14 the brig *Kirkland*: *Evening Star*, March 19, 1859, p. 3.

14 "Collision Off Cove Point": *Evening Star*, Aug. 26, 1865, p.1.

14 the gunboat *Hist*: *Evening Star*, Feb. 20,1908, p.3.

THE DEEP FREEZE AND OTHER HAZARDS

15 revenue cutter *Crawford*: *Evening Star*, Feb. 13, 1895, p. 1.

16 fate of the *Androscoggin*: *The Washington Post*, Jan. 7, 1914, p.10.

16 "imprisoned in the pack ice": Feb. 14, 1912, p. 20.

16 "so far distant": *Evening Star*, May 20, 1912, p.18.

17 on the Bay in recent years: *Baltimore Sun*, Nov. 21, 1920, p. CA7.

THE THREE RIVERS

18 burning from stem to stern: *Baltimore Sun*, July 5, 1924, p.1.

18 since that day: *Sunday Star*, July 6, 1924, p.1.

Notes

THE KEEPER'S LIFE

19 "dressed in a sailor's suit": *Baltimore Sun*, May 6, 1876, p. 4.

20 "The buzzards had eaten": *Baltimore Sun*, Oct. 12, 1880, p. 1.

REAL HAPPINESS

20 Ten barges off Cove Point: "Ten Barges and One Tug," *Baltimore Sun*, July 29, 1913, p. 8.

21 "any old time": "Keeper Daniels 71 Years Old," *Baltimore Sun*, Sept. 9, 1915, p. 7.

21 "drove the carriage": *The Washington Post*, Aug. 30, 1915, p. 4.

21 Daniels died: "Secretary Daniels' Uncle Drops Dead," *Evening Sun*, March 9, 1917, p. 16.

NOT A DESK JOB

22 "none the worse": *Evening Star*, Sept. 23, 1924, p. 1.

22 the summer of 1933: I read the lighthouse logs at the National Archives and Records Administration (NARA) in Washington, D.C. Unfortunately, several logs are missing and neither NARA nor the U.S. Coast Guard professes any knowledge of their whereabouts. According to NARA, the logs maintained at the archives include:

1/1/1903 - 1/1/1909; 1/1//1915 - 1/1/1925;
1/1/1925 - 1/1/1942; 9/1/1952 - 12/1/1953;
1/1/1955 - 11/1/1955; 1/1/1957 - 7/1/1958;
8/1/1958 - 12/1/1959; and 1/1/1960 - 12/1/1970.

23 exhausted carrier pigeon: *Baltimore Sun*, Oct. 9, 1930, p. 25.

23 fatigued carrier pigeon: *Baltimore Sun*, May 9, 1933, p. 19.

CHAPTER 3. THE COVE

page nos.

25 **over $700 in passenger revenue:** "Maryland Delaware & Virginia Railway Company Annual Report, Statement of Freight and Passenger Revenue by Wharves for the Fiscal Year Ending December 31st, 1907." Original in private ownership; copy deposited in collections of Calvert Marine Museum.

25 **backing out from the wharf:** *Baltimore Sun*, Dec. 17, 1913, p. 8.

26 **young Tom Buckler:** *Baltimore Sun*, Aug. 18, 1909, p. 8.

27 **schoolhouse was built:** Mary B. Rockefeller, *Early Schools of Calvert County Maryland*, (2019), pp. 163-166.

A NEW PERSPECTIVE

29 **"how large they grow":** *Baltimore Sun*, Aug. 15, 1915, p. 16.

30 **"within easy reach":** "AROUND CHESAPEAKE BAY," *Baltimore Sun*, June 23, 1918, p. MT2.

30 **"Chesapeake Beach Night Fishing Good":** *The Washington Post*, Aug. 14, 1923, p. 15.

31 **In January, 1935:** "$9,500,000 Negro Colony Planned in Calvert County," *Baltimore Sun*, Jan. 31, 1935, p. 20.

31 **Just two days later:** "Negro Colony Plan Rejected," *Baltimore Sun*, Feb. 2, 1935, p. 20.

500 YARDS OF BAYFRONT? YOURS FOR $2500

32 **"A wonderful value":** p. W4.

33 **Brazilian steamer *Paraense*:** *Baltimore Sun*, Dec. 23, 1862, p.1.

33 **home for six years:** *Calvert Journal*, Feb. 9, 1878, p.1.

35 **"A love affair":** *Baltimore Sun*, Feb. 10, 1916, p.14.

Notes

35 **But old man Hagelin:** Thanks to Leila Boyer, research historian and former director of the Calvert County Historical Society, for providing the happy ending to this story, based on newspaper and U.S. Census records.

36 **great-grandchildren:** "*Post* Carrier G.W. Hagelin Dead at 85," *The Washington Post*, Oct. 19, 1963, p. C3.

THE COVE POINT CLUB

36 **"New Summer Resort":** April 11, 1925, p. 24.

37 **incorporated in the State of Delaware:** The Club's certificate of incorporation, annual reports, and certificate of dissolution were accessed at the Delaware Division of Corporations, Dover, Delaware.

37 **Wilbur Hinman:** Oct. 24, 1960, p. B4.

38 **Hope Peters:** "Hope K. Peters, 83, Yeomanette in Navy," *The Washington Post*, Oct. 19, 1972, p. C4.

A VERY DIFFERENT VISION

39 **killed in auto accidents:** *Calvert Gazette*, July 20, 1929, p. 1.

CHAPTER 4.

THE CUNNING OF J. COOK WEBSTER

40 **descended from John Webster:** Interviews with T. Aaron Horner, Research Assistant, Nabb Research Center for Delmarva History and Culture on his genealogy of Webster descendants on Deal Island, Jan. 22, 2021, and Rev. David Webster, Pastor, St. John's United Methodist Church, Deal Island, Jan. 9, 2021.

41 **general merchandise store:** Kathleen Branch, "The General Stores of Calvert County: Some Are No More on Solomons Island," *Calvert County Recorder*, Dec.18, 1981, p. 1.

43 **Charles' Gift:** *Salute to a Maryland House of 1650*, Hulbert Footner (New York: Harper & Bros., 1939).

OPENING DAY

RACIAL EXCLUSION

THE ROAD COVENANT

COME ON DOWN!

54 **"thing these fish like"**: "Rod and Stream," *Evening Star*, Feb. 7, 1936, p. A15.

54 **"Out Fishin'"**: Oct. 27, 1936, p. X19.

55 **"Fishing Season at its Height"**: "Routes Given to Fishing Grounds in Southern Maryland," *The Washington Post*, Aug. 27, 1922, p. 58.

57 **"delightful new subdivision"**: May 3, 1936, p. R6.

CHAPTER 5. THE LEGEND OF TRYN TRAVA

58 **"reveled in the freedom"**: All of the references to Natalie Scheffer's earlier life in Russia before and after the Bolshevik revolution are from her memoir, written under the pseudonym Natalia Petrova, *Twice Born in Russia* (New York: Wm. Morrow & Co., 1930).

62 **couple left Moscow**: In reporting her death of cardiac arrest at her Washington home on Dec. 11, 1981 ("Natalie P. Scheffer, 91, Author": Dec. 23, 1981, p. B12), *The Washington Post* mistakenly reported that she had left Moscow with her first husband, Prince Nicholas Wolkonsky, and later married Paul Scheffer. She was actually divorced from the prince and married Scheffer before leaving Russia.

AN EXILE "COLONY"

62 **"Russians Make a Play"**: *The Washington Post*, April 21, 1934, p. 13.

63 **"Maslenitsa"**: "Bal Masque to Celebrate Russian Fete," *The Washington Post*, Feb. 26, 1935, p.10.

63 **"Circle of Thirty"**: "Russians Plan Church Benefit," *The Washington Post*, Dec. 1,1935, p. S2.

63 **"Circle of Russians"**: "Russian Church Fair Set for December 13," *Evening Star*, Dec. 1, 1935, p. 28.

63 **Natalie's elder son**: "Choir, Dagger Dance Feature Russian Fair," *The Washington Post*, Dec. 14, 1935, p.2.

78 **at the Library of Congress:** Lubov's colleagues, Serge and Katya Martinoff, also bought four lots at Cove Point, on Elm Drive, which they mowed every summer weekend, but never built a house.

DA SVIDANYA: FAREWELL TO COVE POINT

80 **preservationist moved it:** In 1977, the Calvert County Historical Society authorized Perry Van Vleck to move the chapel to his property in Dunkirk, Maryland, to which he had also moved several other historic buildings. Around 2009, another preservationist, Steuart Chaney, moved the chapel to an historic village operated by the Deale Area Historical Society at Herrington Harbor North, where it was restored, and can be visited by appointment.

CHAPTER 6. THE INVASION

82 **less than twelve hours:** "United States Navy and Marines Descended Upon County in 1942," *Calvert Independent*, (Tercentennial Ed.) Sept. 23, 1954, p. 23.

83 **The dispossessed included:** *Judgment on the Declaration of Taking*, U.S. District Court, Nov. 30, 1942, mdlandrec. net; AAH 49, p. 203.

83 **invasion of Cove Point Beach:** The property the army rented (now 3077 Calvert Boulevard) was owned by Bertha Blake of Arlington, Virginia, who'd bought two waterfront lots from the Websters on July 6, 1937.

THE MARTIN FAMILY

84 **Sisters Kathy and Mary Ellen:** The Martin sisters, later Kathy Martin Wolfe, and Mary Ellen Martin Schultz, shared with me their recollections of the amphibious landing exercises in separate interviews at their homes in Chesapeake Ranch Estates in November 2019.

A BOY AND HIS BIKE

"WAR" IN THE FRONT YARD

BEYOND THE COVE

BACK TO NORMAL

97   **Bob Wilson:** Bob Wilson married Katharine Rebekah Kratz ("Kitty Beck") of Owings, Maryland, who, as a child, had also watched paratroopers descending from the sky for training maneuvers in Calvert County. She was a classmate of Lighthouse Keeper (1943-58) James T. Somers' son "Jimmy T" at school in Prince Frederick.

98   **blown up later:** "Four Rockets Washed Up On Bay Beach," *The Washington Post*, July 30, 1960, p. A3.

CHAPTER 7. THE FIFTIES

99   **A front-page editorial:** Sept. 13, 1945.

100   **"all the sand blowing":** Chuck Miller shared this and many more memories of the Miller and Ryan families' early years at Cove Point, during the course of several telephone interviews.

100   **last craft bookbinders:** Marianne LaRoche, "The Last Bookbinder," *Sunday Star*, Dec. 14, 1969, p. 157.

THE LaPADULAS

102   **Lighthouse Boulevard in 1941:** Karin LaPadula, now living in Seattle, Washington, shared family photos and recollections of her family's early years at Cove Point.

THE TUVE FAMILY

107   **tall, handsome, young man:** Christine Tuve Burris shared photos, documents, and memories of her family's introduction to Cove Point in many conversations at the beach.

THE BRANNANS

110   **how to earn it:** "Four Sons in Mt. Rainier Family Honored on Newspaperboy Day," *Evening Star*, Oct. 7, 1950, p. 11.

110   **family's ninety-minute drive:** Francis ("Frannie") Brannan shared a family photo album while reminiscing about the family's early years at Cove Point, in an interview at his summer home on Holly Drive.

page nos.

111 **"salesmanship":** Gilbert Gimble, "That Housewife's Magic
Recipe Qualifies Her for a Census Job," *Sunday Star*, Jan.
17, 1960, p.23.

CHAPTER 8. THE BOTTOMLESS PIT

113 **"excavating sands":** First lease between the Glascocks and
Charles E. Jefferson, Oct. 21, 1952. Mdlandrec.net: AWR
31, p. 592.

113 **demand in the aircraft industry:** It was reported that only
2,000 tons of the metal was being produced nationwide,
while the Air Force needed 150,000 tons annually.

CATTAIL MARSH

114 **the muskrat season:** "Have Some Muskrat?: A Long-
Ignored Delicacy Coming Into Its Own," *Baltimore Sun*,
May 15, 1910, p.12; "Muskrat Hunting: The Sport Along
the Patuxent Marshes," *Baltimore Sun*, May 2, 1887, p.6;
Lawrence H. Baker, "Muskrat Mysteries Unexplained,"
Baltimore Sun, Feb. 25, 1940, p.MS1.

THE PARTNER

115 **Rogers had been:** "Building Ark in His Back Yard But Not
With Noah's Motive," *Baltimore Sun*, Sept. 28, 1931, p. 3.

115 **A year later:** "Backyard-Built Boat Launched," *Baltimore
Sun*, July 10, 1932, p. 3.

116 **production of ship parts:** "Tiny Shipyard Revolutionizes
Production of Masts and Booms," AP, *Sunday Star*, Sept.
26, 1943, p. 26.

116 **the only headlines:** " Oil drilling operations," *Vidette-
Messenger*, Nov. 7, 1939, p. 4; "Oil Well Gushes Near City
Limits," *Indianapolis News*, Nov. 20, 1939, p. 1; " Files
Demurrer to WPA Charges," *Indianapolis Star*, March
2, 1940, p. 3; "Indianapolis Trio Freed on W.P.A. Fraud
Charge," AP, *Evening Star*, Feb. 7, 1941, p. 13.

Notes

page nos.

116 **Associated Press reported:** "Bay Shore to Be Site of Hunt for Titanium, *Baltimore Sun*, Dec. 19, 1953, p. 41.

117 **Ads for the stock:** *Evening Star*, May 6, 1954, p. 35.

118 **the "wonder metal":** "Titanium Found Along Chesapeake," *The Washington Post*, Jan. 22, 1955, p.20.

119 **Rogers told the press:** "Mining May Aid Farmers: Titanium Firm Also to Produce Liming Materials," *Baltimore Sun*, April 22, 1955, p. 28.

119 **"swamped with leads":** *Evening Star*, Nov. 27, 1955, p. 77.

119 **In March of 1957:** Under this third lease, the rent was to escalate annually, with an option to renew for 15 years with payment of 10% of sales in lieu of rent. Mdlandrec: JLB 13, p. 86.

"IF NOT MORIBUND"

121 **Rogers' improvements intact:** These included an engine, cabin, toilet and bunks installed at a cost to Titanium Ores of $2,854.70.

121 **The court laid the blame:** *Solomons Marina v. Rogers*, 156 A. 2d 432, 221 Md. 194 (1959).

122 **a new agreement:** a fourth lease with Jefferson, at lower rent, was signed April 6, 1959. Mdlandrec: JLB 24, p. 118.

122 **"unable to perform the work":** "Shell Denial By Goldstein: No Firm in Mind For Dredging, He Replies to Byrd," *Baltimore Sun*, Nov. 10, 1959, p. 12.

PROJECT BOOTSTRAP

page nos.

122 **"Report to Stockholders"**: A copy of this report was obtained from the Calvert Marine Museum. Among other things, it included a 1958 report on the "Ore and Shell Content of the Beach Sands at Cove Point, MD." by "Harlan J. Brown, Metallurgical Engineer, Colorado School of Mines," without mentioning that the author had graduated only a year earlier. Mr. Brown's report concluded that the shell plant, with some mechanical changes, could be run for many years at a good profit, and the other minerals (presumably titanium and zircon) could be stockpiled in sufficient quantities "to solve most marketing problems."

"BY THE COMPANY HE KEEPS"

125 **trying to save the S&L**: "Nash Asks Admiral for S&L Details," *The Washington Post*, Feb. 17, 1962, p. B1.

DIGGING DEEPER

126 **"Space Minerals, Inc."**: The Articles of Incorporation were accessed on microfiche at the Maryland State Archives in Annapolis.

CHAPTER 9. THE EYE OF THE STORM

129 **Fonseca**: "Hard Luck Angler is Held as Stowaway," *The Washington Post*, Sept. 6, 1960, p. A3; "Jury Hears Seaman Case," *Baltimore Sun*, Dec. 16, 1960, p. 33; "Sailor Convicted on Entry Count," *Baltimore Sun*, Dec. 20, 1960, p. 32; "Man Jailed in Entry Case," *Baltimore Sun*, Dec. 28, 1960, p. 33.

130 **Cove Point Citizens Association**: interview with Christine Tuve Burris, Sept. 1, 2019.

130 **"Baczenas"**: "Eugene Baczenas, 68, Civil Service Aide, Dies," *Evening Star*, Dec. 9, 1968, p.21.

132 **Joyce Freeland**: telephone interview Jan. 23, 2021.

133 **Michael Kent**: author of *Mulatto: The Black History of Calvert County* (2019); telephone interview Jan. 23, 2021.

page nos.

133 **post-slavery period:** "Negroes in Calvert County, " *Calvert Independent,* Tercentenary Edition, Sept. 23, 1954, p. 23.

135 **Freedom Riders:** Simeon Booker, *Shocking the Conscience: A Reporter's Account of the Civil Rights Movement,* (University Press of Mississippi, 2013).

CHAPTER 10. THE DEVIL'S GRASP

THE FAMILY PICNIC, SEPTEMBER 14, 1947

139 **As reported in the newspapers:** There was wide coverage of the tragedy: "Blanc Drownings," *Minneapolis Star,* Sept. 15, 1947, p. 9; "Diplomat's Wife, Child Drown," *New York Times,* Sept. 15, 1947, p. 18: "Mother and Daughter Drown At Cove Point Lighthouse," *Calvert Independent,* Sept. 18, 1947, p. 4. "Mother Drowns As Attempt To Save Child Fails," *Evening Star,* Sept. 15, 1947, p. 17; "Seas Hamper Search for Body of Girl," *The Washington Post,* Sept. 16, 1947, p. 2B; "Drowning Victim's Body Recovered in Maryland," *Evening Star,* Sept. 22, 1947, p. 17.

THE TWINS, AUGUST 24, 1983

141 **It was a Wednesday:** Author's telephone interviews with Clarissa Sheridan Westenburger, March 24 and 25, 2020.

146 **meticulously detailed report:** Yvonne Heffner, "Rip Tide Batters Six: Near Drownings at Cove Point," *Calvert Recorder,* Aug. 31, 1983, p.1.

THE BROTHERS, JULY 24, 2015

147 **Jason later told:** Jon Woodrow Cox, "Bay current took 2 men by surprise," *The Washington Post,* July 28, 2015, p. B.1.

148 **Less than 100 yards:** Author interviews and correspondence with Shawn Carroll and Ana Giordano, September 2020.

THE WATERMEN

page nos.

150 **If there was one:** Author interviews with Bobby Darnell, September 2020.

THE INCONCEIVABLE

153 **All Oliver was doing:** John Woodrow Cox, "He knew two men had just drowned at Cove Point. He went in the water anyway," *The Washington Post*, Aug. 4, 2015: http://wapo.st/1Ds26j9?tid=ss_mail

153 **His friend Tim:** Author interview with Tim Whitehouse, September 2020.

153 **A woman in a kayak:** Author interviews with Bobby Darnell, September 2020.

CHAPTER 11. BEHEMOTHS ON THE BAY

156 **mixed feelings about it:** Naomi S. Royner, "Environmentalists Find More Gas Sites Than Cove Point," *Baltimore Sun*, April 25, 1972, p. A11; Richard D. Lyons, "Liquid Natural Gas Depot Leaves Area Seemingly Unworried," *New York Times*, April 25, 1978, p. 25.

157 **storage plant explosions:** (AP) *New York Times*, Oct. 21, 1944, p. 19.

WHITE DUST

160 **a joint venture:** the two companies were Raymond Tidewater Construction Corp. of Virginia Beach, Virginia, and Peter Kiewit Sons of Omaha, Nebraska.

160 **One of those workers:** Author's interviews with Roy Hayes in 2019, in which he described his contact with asbestos while working as an insulator during construction of the Calvert Cliffs Nuclear Power Plant, and with other toxic materials while working on the Columbia LNG pipeline. He was undergoing physical therapy for the lung diseases—asbestosis and COPD—discovered when he retired in 2002.

Notes

163 **a heart attack:** Methylene chloride turns into carbon monoxide when inhaled, and can disrupt the oxygen supply to the heart at high doses, even switching off the breathing center of the brain. Mental confusion, lightheadedness, nausea and headache can result from even short-term exposure to high concentrations of the chemical.

163 **scarring of the lungs:** Once the tissues are scarred, the lungs cannot function properly, causing chest pain, coughing, shortness of breath and tightness in the chest.

SHIP AHOY!

165 **terminal's bright future:** "Cove Point LNG Terminal," *Baltimore Sun*, Jan. 3, 1979, p. A14.

EXPLOSION

166 **"It took one gallon":** "Cove Point blast tied to LNG rules," (AP) *Baltimore Sun*, Oct. 16, 1979, p. C2.

168 **failed pump seal:** "Cove Point Explosion Laid to Seal," *Baltimore Sun*, April 17, 1980, p. D1.

SUPPLY AND DEMAND

168 **turned to glut:** Two major pipeline companies that had been buying the gas from drillers along the Appalachian Mountains from Kentucky to Pennsylvania announced in April 1979 that they were oversupplied and not able to buy all they were being offered. This slide from scarcity to surplus had been going on for a decade due in part to federal price regulation of supplies sold across state borders. A lid on prices had dampened any incentive to search for new gas fields. Attention turned instead to abundant resources in countries such as Algeria, although the cost of liquefying the gas for transport from abroad made it more expensive. David Brown, "Gas Producers Suffering from U.S. Policy Shift," *Baltimore Sun*, April 23, 1979, p. A1.

CHAPTER 12. THE EVIL WITHIN

page nos.

170 **three neighborhood boys:** Author's interviews July 2019. To protect the boys' privacy, their real names are not used.

173 **"Child molestation charges filed":** Curt Hules, *Calvert Recorder*, Feb. 12, 1997, p. 1.

173 **pleaded guilty:** Curt Hules, "Guilty Plea in sex case," *Calvert Recorder*, June 20, 1997, p. 1.

174 **supervised release for life:** "Maryland sex offender sentenced to prison for receiving child pornography," News release, Dept. of Homeland Security, ICE, Jan. 24, 2012. https://www.ice.gov/news/releases/maryland-sex-offender-sentenced-prison-receiving-child-pornography#wcm-survey-target-id.

CHAPTER 13. THE GIANT AWAKENS

175 **Robert Southey:** *Poetical works of Robert Southey (1829)*, London: Longman, Brown, Green and Longmans (1853).

175 **Columbia finally gave up:** In 2000, CLNG sold the entire Cove Point operation for $150 million to the Williams Companies, the Tulsa-based operator of a natural gas pipeline system and fiber optic communications business.

176 **With a mutual interest:** Max Ehrenfreund, "The Stakes at Cove Point," *The Washington Post*, Dec. 7, 2014, p. G1.

176 **an export facility:** The 2005 amended agreement allowed Dominion to use the site for "receipt by tanker and the receipt or delivery by pipeline" of natural gas in its various forms. The phrase "delivery by pipeline," the Sierra Club argued, meant pipelines to its domestic customers, not to tankers at Dominion's pier.

CHAPTER 14. THEN AND NOW

page nos.

185   **The Cove Point Lighthouse:** Raymond McCaffrey, "Calvert to Open Up Lighthouse; County Takes Over Cove Point Beacon From Coast Guard," *The Washington Post*, Nov. 2, 2000. p. 3.

187   **flood-mitigation:** The Cove Point Community Flood Mitigation Plan is available online: https://www.calvert-countymd.gov/554/Floodplain-Management

ACKNOWLEDGMENTS

When I learned that *Bay Weekly* founder and long-time publisher Sandra Olivetti Martin and her husband, Bill Lambrecht, recently retired Washington, D.C. correspondent for Hearst Newspapers and the *St. Louis Post-Dispatch*, were now book publishers, I was as excited as a mariner reaching home port after a challenging voyage. No one appreciates the communities along the Chesapeake Bay better than Sandra, and great reporting is Bill's mainstay. I thought they might be as fascinated as I by the stories that made this sand spit called Cove Point such a remarkable landmark on the Bay. And I was right.

New Bay Books also introduced me to artist Suzanne Shelden, well known throughout Maryland for the creativity she brings to every work she touches, which now includes this volume.

Two superb writer/editors, and dear friends, Fredrica Depew and Paul Lagasse, critiqued the first draft of this manuscript, suggesting astute course corrections as well as line-by-line edits. Mary Jo Lazun, an expert at legal research, and Margaret Kingston Waranowitz, meticulous genealogist, helped me through some puzzling mazes. I am also indebted to Robert Hurry, registrar, Calvert Marine Museum; and John Johnson, director, Leila Boyer, research historian and former director, and the staff and volunteers of the Calvert County Historical Society for their invaluable assistance with my research over three years.

Thanks, also, to Kay Trueman Forman, for introducing me to her gracious aunt, Teresa Gibson, who at 90+ years of age shared with me vignettes of life on Solomons Island in the 1930s and '40s; and to Roy Hayes, whose first-person account documents the high price that he and others paid for the privilege of short-term jobs in ventures that changed Calvert County as well as their lives.

I am grateful to the members of the Cove Point Beach community who shared generously of their memories, especially Christine Tuve Burris, who gifted me a treasure trove of photos and documents dating back to her parents' courtship in the Cove in the 1930s. Tracy Stone Doerrer led me to eye-witness accounts of the Army's amphibious landing training from the Martin sisters, whose stories of World War II at Cove Point bring the National Archives' historic photographs to life.

Thanks also to friends Martha Diaz-Ortiz, Susan Andross, Fay Fratz, and Margaret Dunkle whose support has helped to navigate the shoals on this adventure. And, of course, to my son, Teddy, and my late husband, Simeon Booker, a hero to many more than we'll ever know, who taught me how to crack my first steamed crab, cast a line in the surf with a 10-foot pole, clean a seven pound bluefish, and replenish in the peace of the Chesapeake Bay at the end of a rough week.

And finally, my thanks to all who helped to capture the extraordinary history of Cove Point, a worthy landmark on the Chesapeake Bay—a place, to paraphrase the explorer, perfectly framed between heaven and earth.